DENIS BALY

BASIC
BIBLICAL
GEOGRAPHY

FORTRESS PRESS   PHILADELPHIA

Cover: The Dissected Desert. In the distance are the mountains of the Wadi Ram.

Copyright © 1987 by Fortress Press

Library of Congress Cataloging-in-Publication Data

Baly, Denis.
  Basic biblical geography.
  Bibliography: p.
  Includes indexes.
  1. Palestine—Description and travel. 2. Bible—
Geography. 3. Jews—Civilization—To 70 A.D.
I. Baly, Denis. Geography of the Bible. II. Title.
DS104.3.B349   1986   220.9′1   86-45206
ISBN 0-8006-1922-6

2530E86   Printed in the United States of America   1-1922

143051

CONTENTS

INTRODUCTION

This book is designed for students, and I hope many others, who are embarking for the first time on serious biblical study, and who need some preparatory information about the land in which such a very large proportion of biblical events took place. Those readers who know my earlier book, *The Geography of the Bible* (Harper & Row, 1974), now alas out of print, will realize that this present book is in large measure a simplified version, though it has been brought up to date and contains some new material.

What I have tried to do is provide in outline the essential information about the place of Palestine and Transjordan within that much vaster area which we call the Middle East, the structural patterns and the landforms which have helped to determine human movement—armies, migrants, merchants, pilgrims, etc.—as well as the climate upon which all the natural vegetation and the land use depended, and therefore, of course, the daily life of villagers, townspeople, and wandering shepherds and rearers of camels. I have assumed no prior knowledge and have therefore tried to avoid technical terms, and to explain them where they were necessary. Throughout I have had in mind a college or university class, or a parish group, able to devote perhaps two weeks (six sessions) to the subject, and have consequently confined myself within these limits.

I have provided some maps to illustrate both the structure and the various regions and hope that they will prove helpful. But by themselves they are insufficient and the reader ought to have at his or her disposal a good biblical atlas. I have therefore included some of these among the Suggestions for Further Reading at the end of the book. No less essential is a good translation of the Bible, since I have included a large number of biblical references so as to emphasize the importance of geographical studies for understanding the Bible, not only the historical events, but also language of the prophets and other biblical writers. For the frequent biblical quotations within the text I have generally used the Revised Standard Version, which still remains, to my mind, the best of the modern translations.

DENIS BALY

CHAPTER ONE

PALESTINE—
AT THE POINT
OF BALANCE

Palestine, although famous in history, is a very little country. From Dan in the north to Beersheba in the south, the traditional limits of ancient Israelite territory (1 Sam. 3:20; 2 Sam. 3:10; 17:11; 24:2; 1 Kings 4:25) is no more than 125 miles (200 km), and the width from the sea through Jerusalem to the River Jordan only 50 miles (80 km). From the sea to the eastern desert just beyond Rabboth Ammon (modern Amman) is 90 miles (144 km).

Palestine's importance results from its position in what today we call the Middle East. A good world atlas will reveal that two gigantic barriers to easy movement march right across the Old World from west to east. These are (1) the great mountain ranges including the Pyrenees and Alps in Europe; the Pontic and Taurus mountains in Turkey; the Elburz and Zagros in Iran; and the Hindu Kush, Tien Shan, Himalayas, and Tsinling Shan in Central and Eastern Asia; and (2) the vast deserts: the Sahara in North Africa, the Arabian and Persian deserts, and the huge desert belt of southern Russia and Mongolia extending as far as the Great Wall of China. There is, however, this essential difference: In the west the mountain ranges are in the north and the deserts in the south, but in Asia it is the other way round—the deserts are to the north and the mountains to the south. The Middle East is where they cross. The pattern is complicated still more by the presence of the "Five Seas," the Mediterranean, Black, Caspian, and Red seas, and the Persian Gulf. It is the presence of these three great obstacles to easy land movement, crowding closely in

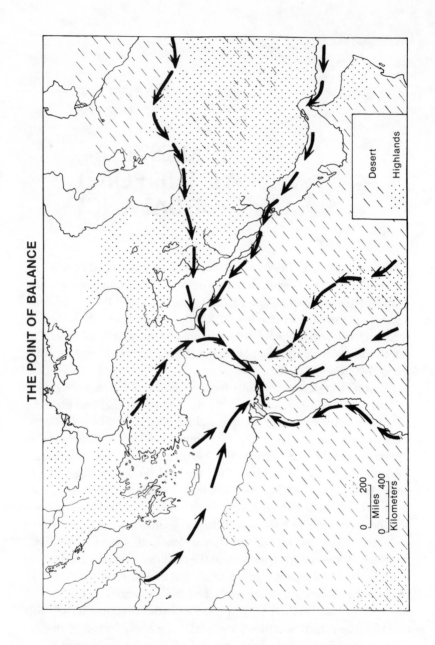

THE POINT OF BALANCE

Desert

Highlands

upon each other, that has given the Middle East its critical importance throughout history.

Palestine lies at a point where this compression is exceedingly acute. Perched at the southwestern end of the "Fertile Crescent" between the Arabian desert and the mountains, it also stands close to Sinai, the narrow land link between Africa and Asia. Merchant caravans and invading armies were bound to penetrate its territory and little could be done to prevent them. When in 333 B.C. Alexander the Great defeated the Persians at Issus, the Middle East became indissolubly linked with Europe, and Palestine was more than once thereafter a beachhead for Western penetration. At no point in its history, with the possible exception of the reign of King David (1000–965 B.C.), was Israel ever free to pursue an independent foreign policy.

THE FERTILE CRESCENT

The Fertile Crescent is that sickle of land, north of the great Arabian desert, where there is sufficient water for agriculture and therefore for settlement in towns and villages. It is bounded on the west by the Mediterranean Sea, and on the north and east by high mountain ranges. To the north is the Armenian mountain knot, the junction of modern Turkey and Iran, and to the east is the towering wall of the Zagros Mountains dividing the lowlands of Iraq from the high plateau country of Iran.

The eastern section of the Fertile Crescent is territory that today we call Iraq, with a moderate supply of rain in the north and a desert climate in the south. Had this been all, the region could have supported only a small population but it is fed also by two great rivers, the Tigris and the Euphrates, which provide plentiful water for irrigation. There is a marked difference between northern and southern Iraq. The north was ancient Assyria where, although the two rivers were the major arteries, winter rainfall made towns and villages away from the rivers possible. To the south was the land of Babylon, low-lying and drawing on the two great rivers for irrigation, but subject to severe spring flooding when the melting snow on the mountains poured down into the lowland. Southern Babylon contains vast areas of marshland with a culture all of its own.

THE FERTILE CRESCENT

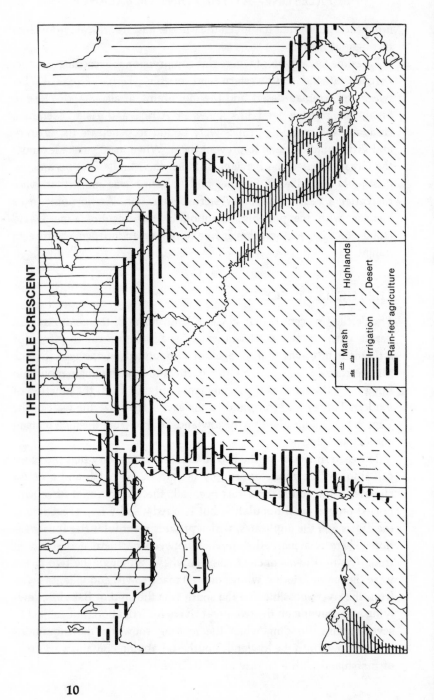

Marsh ||| Highlands

Irrigation / Desert

Rain-fed agriculture

PALESTINE—AT THE POINT OF BALANCE

Babylon and Assyria were the two great imperial powers of the Fertile Crescent throughout all the early years of the Old Testament, and the great rival for power was Egypt. Only in 539 B.C., when Cyrus the Great of Persia conquered Babylon, did control of the Fertile Crescent pass into the hands of a foreign power. In 333 B.C. Alexander of Macedon in Greece defeated Persia at the Battle of Issus and thus began the first European domination of the Middle East. This lasted, however, for only ten years and after the death of Alexander in 323 the old struggle between Egypt and Iraq was renewed, this time between the Ptolemies and the Seleucids. European domination began again when Pompey conquered Syria in 63 B.C., and although constantly opposed by the Parthians and later the Sassanids from their base in Persia and Iraq, this control endured for seven hundred years until the Muslim forces from Arabia won the Battle of the Yarmuq in A.D. 636. Jerusalem surrendered to them peacefully in 637.

The bone of contention was the western section of the Fertile Crescent bordering on the Mediterranean Sea and commonly known today as the Levant,[1] i.e., Syria, Lebanon, Jordan, and Israel, as much a strife-torn region in the ancient past as it is, alas, today. It is within the Levant, and especially in the southern part of it, that most of biblical history was played out, and therefore we must examine it in greater detail.

THE LEVANT

The settled area of the Levant stretches for some 400 miles (640 km) from the foot of the northern mountains to the southern end of the Dead Sea, which is the line where the coast turns westward toward Egypt. From the Dead Sea to the Red Sea at the Gulf of Aqabah is about another 100 miles (160 km), making 500 miles (800 km) in all. It is structurally a very complex region and forms the northernmost extension of an extremely complicated system of gigantic clefts in the earth's surface, extending as far as the northern frontier of South Africa. Throughout the greater part of East Africa there are two enor-

---

1. The term "Levant" in earlier years included all the eastern Mediterranean, but tends today to be restricted to the countries mentioned.

mous Rift Valleys, with the Red Sea forming a third. In the Levant there is only one, most clearly visible in the north-south Jordan Valley and the dry Arabah from the Dead Sea to Aqabah.

Generally speaking, the Levant consists of four north-south zones: the *Coast Plain*, the *Western Highlands*, the *Central Rift Valley*, and the *Eastern Plateau*. The picture is a great deal more complicated than that, however. In addition to the very evident north-south pattern there is also another, from northeast to southwest, most clearly visible in the Lebanon-Syria region immediately north of Palestine. Both these lines are accompanied by others at right angles to them, so that the whole Levant region is marked by a network of cleavages and parallel highlands: north-south/east-west and NE-SW/NW-SE.

These two patterns tend to alternate with each other. Thus the northeast-southwest line is most clearly dominant in the extreme north beside the Iskanderan Gulf and then again further south in the Lebanon and Anti-Lebanon mountains, while the north-south line dominates in the Nuseiriyeh Mountains along the coast of northern Syria and in the Palestine region to the south.

Separating these alternate northeast-southwest and north-south zones are a number of long depressions running from west to east, not always easily visible on an atlas map but of great cultural importance. These are

a. The Aleppo-Euphrates Depression in the extreme north, clearly evident in the sudden turn of the River Euphrates eastward;

b. The Homs-Palmyra Corridor, which may be traced all the way eastward to the borders of Iran;

c. The Galilee-Bashan Depression running eastward from the Bay of Acco to the Lake of Galilee and the Valley of the Yarmuq. It is, however, complicated in places by great outflows of basalt and by another depression running southeast from Sidon;

d. The Beersheba-Zered Depression, which includes Beersheba, the southern end of the Dead Sea, and the Wadi Hesa (biblical River Zered), dividing the ancient territories of Moab and Edom.

Surprising as it may seem to the modern mind accustomed to rapid transport along smooth roads, these long west-east depressions, often unimpressive to the traveler, formed in the past quite definite divisions between the territories on either side of them, as did also of

THE PATTERN OF THE LEVANT

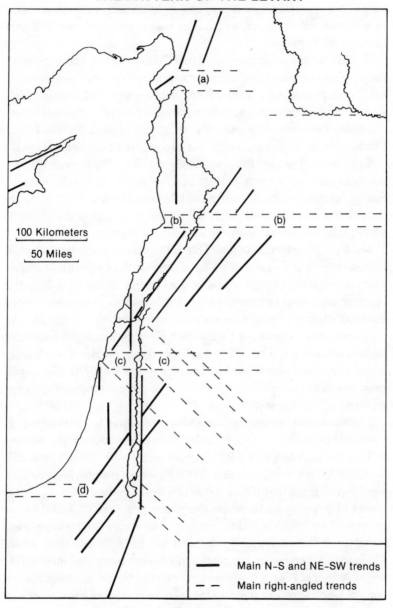

100 Kilometers

50 Miles

(a)

(b)   (b)

(c) (c)

(d)

—— Main N–S and NE–SW trends

- - - Main right-angled trends

course the far more profound depression of the great Central Rift Valley. We may therefore distinguish eight distinct realms, each with its own cultural character, a character that in many of them still persists today. They are:

The Northern Realm. Here the Coast Plain is narrow and somewhat cut off from the interior. It includes the ancient town of Ugarit, important in the Bronze Age. Behind it rise the Nuseiriyeh Mountains, cleft by deep and narrow gorges. Covered by thick forest in ancient times, it is today the home of the Nuseiris, an offshoot from orthodox Islam. The central valley is here much less pronounced than further south, and in the northern section exceedingly marshy. The Eastern Plateau nowhere rises to a great height, and being so far north, receives enough winter rain for cultivation of wheat and barley and pasture for sheep and goats. Unquestionably the dominant section of this realm, it was in Old Testament times the kingdom of Hamath.

The Syro-Phoenician Realm. This is the master realm of the entire Levant. Here the mountains on both sides of the Central Rift Valley reach their greatest height, surpassing 8,000 feet (2,438 m) in both the Lebanon and Anti-Lebanon, and the Rift itself is everywhere more than 3,000 feet (914 m) above sea level. Along the exceedingly narrow and sometimes nonexistent Coast Plain were the wealthy Phoenician ports, such as Tyre, Sidon, Berytus (Beirut), and Byblos (Gebal) from which comes our word "Bible." Trading across the entire Mediterranean and drawing upon the rich forests of the mountains, they were all famous for their wealth.

The mountains themselves were places of refuge from invading armies, and the homes of fiercely independent separatist groups, as they still are today. The Central Rift, known today as the Beqa'a, has rich farmland in its southern section, but it by no means provides the easy north-south route that the map would suggest, for the southern end is blocked by tumbled hills where two fault systems meet, and the northern end by rough volcanic country. All major land routes were therefore deflected round to the east of the Anti-Lebanon, where Damascus, abundantly supplied with water from the mountains, reigns supreme. Whoever wishes to command the Levant must always control Damascus. But it is far from easy to command the Levant and for only ninety years in all the millennia of its long history has

Damascus ever governed a great empire (A.D. 661–750), for she is isolated in her splendor, a glorious oasis and caravan city, but lacking in manpower to create great armies.

The Palestine Realm. Here, because of a major transverse fault cutting across at the foot of Mount Hermon, the Central Rift suddenly drops to its most profound depths and for the longer part of its course before reaching Aqabah is well below sea level. The great trench it has created effectively divides the hills and valleys of Cisjordan (Palestine) from the high tableland of Transjordan. This realm is, of course, the heartland of biblical history, and the one, therefore, to which we shall have to devote most of our attention.

It is in Cisjordan that the Coast Plain becomes for the first time a major feature, widening out south of Mount Carmel, first into the once-marshy Plain of Sharon and then further south into the wide and partly hilly area that became the home of the Philistines.

The Western Highlands descend in two great steps to the low-lying Valley of Jezreel, which connects the coast at Acco (Acre) with the Jordan Valley at Beth-shan. To the south of this the mountains rise again to the true heartland of ancient Israel: Manasseh, Ephraim, and Judah. It is important to notice at this point that the *structural* trend of the mountains here is from southwest to northeast and that therefore the Judean highlands around Jerusalem, Bethlehem, and Hebron are continued across the Jordan Rift in the Dome of Gilead (modern Ajlun Highlands) to the *northeast.* The highlands of Manasseh, which seem to continue the Judean highlands so smoothly, are in fact an uplifted structural *basin* and therefore readily open to invasion.

The Realm of the Southland. The Coast Plain continues, and the Western Highlands drop down just north of Beersheba to the very much lower upland country of the central Negev, which surpasses 3,000 feet (914 m) only in the Har Ramon dome but for much of its length attains little more than 2,000 feet (610 m). The Central Rift Valley climbs gradually to somewhat over 650 feet (198 m) above sea level about 50 miles (80 km) south of the Dead Sea before descending again gradually to sink below the Red Sea at Aqabah. All this region is desert or semidesert. The northwestern section, it is true, is dotted with wells and seems to have been sheep and barley country from a very early date, but south of this there are extensive sand dunes. As the land rises toward the central ridge a narrow zone, no more than 5 miles (8 km) wide, receives heavy dew and occasional, though very erratic, rainfall averaging only 6 inches (150 mm) a year. During the Israelite monarchy there were small settlements here and in the New Testament period the Nabateans built cities to protect the caravan routes leading to Gaza. Immediately the central ridge is crossed, however, the eastern slopes and Rift Valley of the Arabah receive only minimal rain and near-desert conditions prevail.

The Eastern Plateau is markedly different. Rising in precipitous sandstone cliffs to more than 5,000 feet (1,524 m) above sea level it towers above the Arabah. The severe winter storms provide enough water to make possible a line of towns and villages along the plateau edge, the home in the Old Testament of the kingdom of Edom and in the New Testament of the powerful Nabateans, with their capital in the great rock-cut city of Petra. This is beyond question the dominant region of the southland which the Nabateans, and apparently at times also the Edomites, directly controlled. It is, however, a very narrow strip of cultivable land and cannot support a large population. Therefore, it "exported men," as did also the narrow coastland of Phoenicia, sending their sons to earn their living in the distant corners of the world. They were the great traders of the Levant and from their knowledge of the vast world beyond their homes Edom and Tyre became famous for both their wisdom and their arrogance (Jer. 49:7, 16; Ezek. 28:2, 3).

Each of the different regions of the Levant has its own distinct character and way of life, setting it apart from the others. Integration and mutual cooperation, therefore, did not come easily and often collapsed altogether. This strong regional self-consciousness and often mutual suspicion has so marked the Levant throughout its history that lasting political unity has come only from some foreign power, from imperial Rome or Arabian Islam.

EARTHQUAKES

The cracking of the earth's surface that produced the great rifting of the Levant still continues on a very modest scale and small fissures may sometimes happen, though very rarely. Slight earth tremors are common and major earthquakes seem to occur about once every 150 or 200 years, the last one having done appalling damage in Upper Galilee on January 1, 1837. The great earthquake in the days of King Uzziah remained long in Israelite memory (Amos 1:1; Zech. 14:15; and perhaps also Isa. 9:10), and earthquakes are also associated with Elijah's experience in the southern desert (1 Kings 19:11) and with the crucifixion of Jesus (Matt. 15:38), although many scholars are dubious about this last, believing it to be a later addition to the story. (See also Num. 16:30–31; Pss. 18:7; 29:6.)

MAJOR ROCK TYPES IN PALESTINE
AND TRANSJORDAN

In contrast to the structure, these are relatively simple. At the bottom is the hard *granite platform* of Arabia, which here is exposed only in the mountains of Midian in the extreme south of Transjordan, just north of Aqabah.

Above this is the immensely thick *Nubian sandstone*, usually red, but sometimes white, yellow, or purple. This is a major rock of Transjordan, especially in Edom and along the eastern side of the Dead Sea. In Palestine it is found only in a small patch a few miles north of the Red Sea.

Cenomanian limestone is a hard rock, normally white in color but occasionally yellow or reddish. It is the major rock of the mountains of Palestine, as well as the Ajlun (Gilead) Mountains of Transjordan. It is an excellent building stone.

Above this is the *Senonian chalk* and above this again the *Eocene* (either limestone as in Galilee, or chalk as in parts of the southern desert). Chalk is usually soft and easily eroded. The soil is less fertile than that of the limestone, but it is more easily plowed. Because of its softness it tends to form valleys between the harder limestone hills, and it has a smooth surface. Many of the major Palestinian roads follow these soft chalk valleys. The much-harder limestones weather into a rich, often red, soil, and being porous, absorb the winter rain and pay it out in the long summer drought, justifying the description of Palestine as "a good land, a land of brooks of water, of fountains and springs, flowing forth in valleys and hills" (Deut. 8:7). Once thickly forested, the Cenomanian limestone today supports the major olive groves.

The lowlands of the Coast Plain, the Valley of Jezreel, and the Rift Valley are floored with alluvium, a very rich soil, where there is sufficient water (Jezreel is "the rich valley" of Isa. 28:1). The Coast Plain south of Mount Carmel has important areas of red sandy soil, once of little importance, but today noted for their orange groves.

CHAPTER TWO

CLIMATE
AND WEATHER

THE BASIC FACTORS

By the term "climate" we mean the general pattern of temperature, rain or snow, dry periods, etc., which can be expected to recur faithfully year by year in steady succession. This is not, however, static, for we now have sufficient evidence to be certain that climate does in fact fluctuate over the centuries. We can, for instance, be reasonably certain that in Western Europe there have been since 10,000 B.C. prolonged cold and wet periods, lasting several centuries, alternating with warmer, drier periods. Our knowledge of these comes from the evidence of advancing and retreating glaciers, tree rings, as well as documentary evidence of good and bad harvests, severe storms, unusual cold and heat, etc., going back for about nine hundred years, and actual climatic records kept over the last three centuries.

Unfortunately, such evidence for the Levant is still only minimal, and though we may be assured that the climate must have fluctuated, perhaps severely, we cannot as yet say how great these fluctuations were or how long they lasted. We must be on our guard, therefore, against assuming what archaeologists took for granted nearly thirty years ago, that the Palestinian climate has not noticeably changed in four thousand years. We know for certain that it must have done but we cannot as yet describe these changes. Recently the evidence has been beginning to build up and perhaps by the turn of the century we may be able to construct a reliable picture. For the moment all we can do is to describe the modern climate, remembering that conditions may have been different in the monarchy of David and Solomon or the time of Jesus. The general pattern was certainly the same, but whether the winter cold was more severe or the rainfall more assured we do not know.

"Weather" is the term we use for day-to-day conditions, and although the climatic pattern, together with the soil conditions, dictates whether a district is suitable for wheat, barley, olives, or vine, it is the weather of a particular year that determines whether "the valleys deck themselves with grain, they shout and sing together for joy" (Ps. 65:13), or whether people "are ashamed and confounded and cover their heads, because of the ground which is dismayed, since there is no rain on the land" (Jer. 14:3–4). The utterly unexpected can sometimes happen. In 1938 in Edom I experienced a slight shower of rain in the normally absolute drought of June, and in February 1950 snow covered the date palms at Jericho, 1,000 feet (305 m) below sea level.

THE CLIMATE OF THE LEVANT

Four major factors dominate the climate of the Levant. These are

a. The alternating northward and southward movement of the major climatic belts between summer and winter as the sun is overhead, first at the Tropic of Cancer (23.5° N of the equator) and then at the Tropic of Capricorn (23.5° S);

b. The fact that at the southeastern corner of the Mediterranean the desert and the sea come very near to each other;

c. The closeness of the Levant to the great deserts of Arabia and the adjacent Sahara, with their intense summer heat, and the relative closeness of the Russo-Siberian plains, with their very severe winter cold;

d. The fact that the major lines of mountains and deep valleys run more or less from north to south, i.e., directly across the path of the cyclonic storms that move from west to east along the Mediterranean Sea, bringing with them the life-giving rain of winter.

The result of the interaction of these four factors is that there are two dominant seasons: summer and winter, separated from each other by two shorter transitional periods. Although it is convenient to speak of these as the spring and autumn, this is misleading because it suggests something similar to the more prolonged spring and fall with which we are familiar in most of the U.S.A. and Western Europe. "Winter" is also a deceptive word since for us it inevitably suggests severe cold, which in the Levant does not normally occur until January. For the Middle Easterner winter is above all the time of the life-giving rain, and indeed in Arabic the same word, *shittah*, is used for both "winter" and "rain." To keep these important distinctions clearly before us, it will be helpful to speak of the dry season and wet season, and of the spring transition and autumn transition.

Because of its position at the southeastern end of the Mediterranean and also because of the general north-south direction of the mountain ranges it is possible to lay down certain absolute rules for the rainfall distribution:

a. The amount of rain and the length of the rainy period is greater in the north than in the south. Thus Antioch in the extreme north has an average annual rainfall of over 40 inches (1,000 mm) and no absolutely dry month although winter is much wetter than summer, but Beersheba in southern Palestine has only 8 inches (200 mm) with absolute drought for five months in summer.

b. Rainfall is always greater on the western, or seaward, side of any mountain or hill than it is on the eastern side.

c. Evaporation is always greatest on the slopes most exposed to the sun, i.e., on the southern slopes. The result of (a) and (b) combined is that vegetation is always richer and the land in winter greener on the northern and western slopes than it is on the southern and eastern ones. This becomes increasingly marked as one proceeds south and consequently may be observed on every little hillock, however tiny. Where the Transjordan plateau grades off into the desert even the slightest increase in the gentle downward slope causes a decrease in the rainfall, which may often be observed even with the naked eye.

THE DRY AND WET SEASONS

Although the general pattern of the climate remains true for the whole Levant, it will be better during the rest of this chapter to concentrate on Palestine and Transjordan, since this is the area with which most of biblical history is concerned.

The *dry season* is exceedingly regular, starting on about June 15 and ending on about September 15, and during this period day after day is the same. On the Coast Plain during the early hours there is almost complete calm and sunrise brings sudden and exhausting heat. But about 9:00 A.M. the cooler sea breeze begins. The wind slowly increases in strength and the maritime air builds up until, shortly after midday, it overflows the central mountain ridge and pours down like a torrent into the Rift Valley. The Eastern Plateau remains very hot (about 86° F, 30° C) during the day, but around 4:00 P.M. the cooling maritime air suddenly arrives, shaking all the doors and windows. By its steady flow the village farmer winnows the grain, tossing it up in the air to allow the wind to drive away the chaff.

This prolonged drought and heat is certainly the summer's most characteristic feature but it should in no way be exaggerated. Except on the admittedly humid Coast Plain, which, however, enjoys the cooling sea breeze, it is everywhere very dry heat where even the narrow shade of a single column offers immediate relief. On the central mountains of Palestine and the still higher Transjordan plateau the temperature drops suddenly after sunset and the nights are decidedly chilly, with a strong breeze and temperatures normally in the fifties Fahrenheit. The moist heat of the coastal cities can certainly be unpleasant but in general the summer climate is much less exhausting than that of most of the U.S.A. in the same season. Only in the Rift Valley, where the winds are warmed by their sudden descent so that the minimum temperature is a little over 70° F (21° C), does the summer climate merit the term "unbearable."

The *wet season*, in strong contrast to the very regular dry season, is totally unpredictable. No one can ever foretell when it will start, when it will end, how much rain there will be, where it will fall, or how it will be distributed through the season. "Who knows," asked Elihu concerning God's control of the rain and snow, "whether for correction, or for his land, or for love, he causes it to happen?" (Job 37:13, but see the whole chapter).

The rainy season begins in the middle of October, sometimes, as in 1938, with storms of heavy rain throughout the entire cultivated area and even beyond, but more often gradually with scattered showers or thunderstorms, causing "rain upon one city and . . . no rain upon another city" (Amos 4:7). Sometimes, however, the early storms are deceptive, bringing with them no more than "clouds and wind without rain," mere "waterless clouds, carried along by winds" (Prov. 25:14; Jude 12). The people long desperately for rain to come after the five-month drought, since without it the farmers cannot plant their fields and the cisterns, even in severe years the springs, dry up. When "there is no rain on the land, the farmers are ashamed, they cover their heads" (Jer. 14:4). In some years the first rains may be delayed until December or even later, and unless the rain when it finally comes is sufficient the wide area of marginal land, and even much of the better land, fails to produce the desperately needed crops.

Distribution through the season is also important. The winter storms moving in from the Mediterranean usually cause three days of exceedingly heavy rain—continuous and torrential on the first two days, and shorter, but no less torrential, showers on the third day. In a really good year the storms succeed each other with surprising regularity once a week, but normally they are more widely spaced. A particularly disastrous situation occurs when the first storm brings plentiful rainfall but is then succeeded by two or three months with no rain. In such a case the farmer plows his fields and plants his seed in the well-watered soil, only to see them wither and die for lack of further water. Then, when the season's rain comes in earnest, he is left with no grain to plant—except the grain kept aside to feed his family. Crops must, of course, be produced if there is to be food for the following year, and so it was in such situations that the Israelite farmers of the Old Testament were sometimes driven to sell their children into slavery, having no other means of keeping them alive.

Other dangers of the rainy season are hail, snow, and flash floods. Hail may occur anywhere in one of the severe thunderstorms, but it could be especially damaging on the Coast Plain in midwinter. Cold, damp air moving in from the sea and forced to rise rapidly over the still warm land can easily become "a storm of hail, a destroying tempest" (Isa. 28:2). It is only rarely, however, that it attains the savagery of the freak storm in the Valley of Ajalon when "the Lord threw down great stones from heaven upon them as far as Azekah, and they died; there were more who died because of the hailstones than the men of Israel killed with the sword" (Josh. 10:11). On May 23, 1957, at the last gasp of the rainy season, hail "the size of small apples" fell again in the same region.[1]

Snow occurs about every five years on the mountains of Palestine but more frequently on the high plateau of Transjordan, where it falls every year on the highlands of Ajlun (ancient Gilead) and of Edom. On the much-higher mountains of the Jebel Druze in the extreme southeast of Syria and the towering Lebanon and Anti-Lebanon it remains throughout the coldest months, lasting in places until June, and in fact lingers through all the dry summer in the sheltered crevices of Mount Hermon. It may also fall quite heavily, though very rarely, on the Palestine coast plain.

Snow, therefore, may fall at Christmas despite the denials one finds in some books, but it does not often do so, normally occurring later in the year. In fact the Easter ceremonies in Jerusalem are more likely to be conducted in a snow-covered city than the Christmas ceremonies in Bethlehem. March is indeed a very probable month for snow on the Transjordan plateau, and even, though more seldom, the first week in April. This is because the movement of the great pressure systems in the transitional period of the year may leave the way open for a great mass of very cold air to move southward from the frigid plains of Russia.

Flash floods are usually the result of exceptionally heavy rain falling upon dry land with little or no vegetation to hold the soil. They are, therefore, a feature of mountainous desert country where damp air moving in from the sea over the hot highlands is forced to rise rapidly over the barren and superheated soil, causing very heavy rain. Erosion on such occasions is sudden and furious, and gigantic boulders are tumbled down the valley as if they were playthings. The road from the Edomite plateau to the Red Sea at Aqabah, confined as it is between towering cliffs on either side, is especially subject to this savagery of nature. Flash floods, however, are not altogether confined to the desert and semidesert world. About forty years ago such a flood killed a number of people in the Tiberias region.

---

1. J. Katsnelson, "The Frequency of Hail in Israel," *Israel Journal of Earth Sciences* 16 (1967): 1–4.

The *transitional seasons* are each only about six weeks long—from September 1 to mid-October, and from mid-April to the end of May. They are sharply divided from the dry season and merge into the wet season—rain may occur during these intermediate periods. The postsummer season includes the "High Days and Holidays" of the Jewish calendar: Rosh ha-Shanah (New Year) on the first two days of the month of Tishri;[2] Yom Kippur (Day of Atonement), a day of solemn penitence concluding the ten days of repentance with which the new year begins; and Succoth, the Feast of Booths (or Tents), a seven-day celebration starting on the fourteenth day of Tishri. In ancient Israel it was the vintage festival celebrating the annual miracle of the vine, the deep-rooted plant that continues to grow through all the waterless months of the dry season. As the other vegetation dies wild animals become desperate for food and will raid the vineyards, and so farmers camped out in booths or tents to drive off "the foxes, the little foxes that spoil the vineyards" (Song of Sol. 2:15), a practice which was still common well within living memory. On the last day of the feast, when the Temple still stood in Jerusalem, the High Priest would empty a vessel of water on the altar to indicate that the cisterns were running dry and that God alone could send the much-needed rain.

During the transitional season of April and early May the rainfall decreases rapidly and May is normally a totally dry month. It is climatically an unsettled period, however, and in the deserts of southern Palestine, the Arabah, and the Eastern Plateau most of the year's rain may sometimes come in a sudden torrential storm at this end of the season when the overheated land creates rapidly rising air currents. Such storms are sharply limited in extent and the land beyond the edge of the storm remains absolutely dry. This was the situation in the time of Elisha when the kings of Israel and Judah, encamped in the dry valley of the upper Zered between Moab and Edom, saw neither wind nor rain, but "the next morning, about the time of offering the sacrifice, behold, the water came from the direction of Edom, till the country was filled with water" (2 Kings 3:20, but see the whole story in vv. 4–27. I have myself seen something similar in exactly the same region.).

---

2. The Jewish calender follows the phases of the moon and so is not in step with the secular sun calendar.

The two transitional seasons are also the time of the sirocco,[3] "a hot wind from the bare heights in the desert . . . not to winnow or cleanse" (Jer. 4:11), i.e., useless for winnowing the grain. It is a savagely hot desert wind causing a steep rise in temperature of 16°–22° F (9°–12° C) and a sudden drop in relative humidity of as much as 40 percent. The excessive heat and dryness, together with a yellow haze of fine dust, are intensely irritating, and even mild-mannered people lose their temper for no apparent reason. The farther east one goes, the more savage is the sirocco, and to leave the shelter of a building in the eastern desert is to step into a furnace. It is also severe in the Rift Valley where it is further warmed by descent.

On the coast the sea breeze may give some relief, but where the mountains come close to the coast the sirocco may pour down at 60 miles (96 km) an hour or more, rousing the sea to fury. "The east wind has wrecked you in the heart of the seas," said Ezekiel concerning Tyre (Ezek. 27:26). From such a descending torrent a harbor offers no protection. "By the east wind thou didst destroy the ships of Tarshish" (Ps. 48:7). On the highlands the sirocco is seldom a powerful wind and its usually sudden end is immediately evident from the strong west wind that takes its place. All the doors bang at once, the trees toss and sway, and "there is a sound of abundance of rain" (1 Kings 18:41, KJV), for especially in autumn the new west wind often brings heavy rain with it.

The destructive and profitless character of the sirocco, the "fierce blast in the day of the east wind" (Isa. 27:8), is a persistent biblical theme indicating the impermanence of riches and of human life, "for the wind passes over it, and it is gone, and its place knows it no more" (Ps. 103:16). "All flesh is grass, and all its beauty is like the flower of the field. The grass withers, the flower fades, when the breath of the Lord blows upon it" (Isa. 40:6–7). "Though he may flourish as the reed plant," said Hosea of the ruler of the Northern Kingdom, "The east wind, the wind of the Lord, shall come, rising from the wilderness; and his fountain shall dry up, his spring shall be parched; it shall strip his treasury of every precious thing" (Hosea 13:15).[4]

---

3. Also sometimes called *khamsin*, but this is an Egyptian term and is better kept for that country where conditions are different.

4. See also Job 37:16–17; Ezek. 17:10; Hosea 12:1; Luke 12:55; James 1:11.

CHAPTER THREE

LIFE
IN ANCIENT
PALESTINE

THE THREEFOLD PATTERN OF
ISRAELITE LIFE

During the last hundred years or so it has been common to divide the people of the ancient Levant into three distinct groups: the sedentary *farmers*, tilling the soil; the wandering *Bedouin*, with their camels, sheep, and goats; and the *merchants*, deriving their wealth from trade. In recent years, however, this concept has been seriously questioned, some scholars going so far as to reject it altogether. In general, however, the distinction seems sound. Indeed, right up to very recent times it still existed east of the Jordan although there also it was beginning to disappear. The error of the earlier scholars was (1) that they often took it for granted that the three groups developed in succession to each other in a Darwinian fashion, herders coming first, then farmers, and finally merchants;[1] and (2) that they tended very often to treat the separation between these three groups as absolute. It is now clear, however, that the three types of society did not evolve out of each other but that all began in a primitive and tentative form about ten thousand years ago as attempts to cope with the problem of an in-

---

1. I remember a distinguished professor in the early 1930s insisting that he could as easily believe that the sun had risen in the west and set in the east as he could believe in an agricultural society which had not previously gone through the hunting and gathering and then pastoral stages.

creasing population but a decreasing food supply. Jericho in the lower Jordan Valley and Çatal Hüyük on the Anatolian plateau of central Turkey both seem to have come into existence as trading settlements rather than as farming communities, although of course they did cultivate the land close to them.

The primary necessity of the farmer was *stability* and also a sufficiency of water to enable the crops to grow and ripen. "A king is an advantage to a land with cultivated fields" (Eccles. 5:9)[2] for it was essential that the farmer and his family should remain on the land, cultivating it and caring for it from one generation to another, and for this he needed the protection of a strong government. Only the "prodigal son" would desert the family heritage, and the elder brother in the parable had serious reason for his complaint (Luke 15:11-24). Moreover, the farmer required the security of clearly defined boundaries so that others would not trespass upon his carefully cultivated land. Altering one of these boundaries secretly in the dark of the night was one of the abominable acts listed in Deuteronomy for "cursed be he who removes his neighbor's landmark" (Deut. 27:17), and again, "Remove not the ancient landmark which your fathers have set" (Prov. 22:28). When the central government was weak or corrupt "caravans ceased and travelers kept to the byways. The peasantry ceased in Israel" (Judges 5:6-7).

The shepherd, however, required *mobility*, the freedom to move over wide areas in search of good pasture, and for him such boundaries were an irritant and an obstacle. Certainly this freedom of movement was not absolute and each group had its own grazing grounds, which would be defended, if necessary, by force. In the true deserts to the east the flocks and herds would be taken to where it had rained, a subject of constant discussion in the tents, but in most of the area with which we are concerned the tribal movements tended to be "transhumant," traveling regularly every year between the same winter and summer pastures, e.g., from the warm Rift Valley in winter to the cooler plateau country in summer. A transhumant movement which continued until the war of 1967 made it impossible was that of a

---

2. The Hebrew of this sentence is obscure and its translation much disputed. Interpretations vary widely.

LIFE IN ANCIENT PALESTINE

Bedouin group near Petra in Edom who moved each year to and from the pastureland east of Bethlehem.

The merchant needed both *mobility* and *stability*, for the roads along which he traveled could only too easily be raided unless they had government protection. His home was in the town rather than the village and there his family remained. Merchants became by far the wealthiest of the three groups, and their ruthless treatment of the often poverty-stricken peasants was much condemned by the prophets:

> They covet fields, and seize them;
>   and houses, and take them away;
> they oppress a man and his house,
>   a man and his inheritance.
>   (Micah 2:2)

All three types of life existed from the very beginnings of permanent human settlement ten thousand years ago, and although it would be false to speak of organized trade at so early a date, there was certainly an exchange of products over enormous distances. Obsidian from the volcanic mountains of central Turkey was brought to pre-pottery Jericho despite the towering and then thickly forested mountain ranges between them, and the recently discovered pre-pottery settlement at 'Ain Ghazzal near Amman in Jordan was in contact with northern Iraq.

In course of time, society and culture became more complex as a result of foreign influence and penetration, either by peaceful migration or by invasion and war, from which the area is little protected by natural barriers. The interdependence of the three groups consequently became both more intricate and more essential. Much of the interchange of products and other business took place outside the town gate, and the judges sat there to adjudicate disputes (Amos 5:10, 12), but the interrelationship was more complex than that. Many small villages included both farmers and herders, since they were on the edge of the cultivable land. The transhumant pastoralists often regularly provided animals to assist with plowing at the beginning of the rainy season or threshing the grain at its end. The merchants depended both upon the animals for transport and upon their owners as drivers and guides. For many millennia these animals were only donkeys since the camel did not, apparently, come into full use until the period of the monarchy, i.e., after about 1000 B.C. With the establishment of the monarchy the semidesert and desert people were the source of sheep and lambs for the temple sacrifices and wool for clothing (2 Kings 3:4; see also Prov. 31:13; Ezek. 34:3; Hosea 2:5, 9).

PALESTINIAN FARMING

Beyond question, the foundation of Israelite society was the farming community, although, as we shall see in chapter 5, conditions were different on the Eastern Plateau. The three major feasts—the "feast of unleavened bread" in early April, the "feast of harvest" seven weeks later, and the "feast of ingathering at the end of the year," i.e., the grape harvest—were all agricultural feasts (Exod. 23:14-16; see also 34:18-24). The Passover seems to have been incorporated into the feast of unleavened bread during the reign of Josiah in the latter part of the monarchy.

Even in the early Bronze Age, about 2400 B.C., the woodlands and forest on the central highlands were being felled as the need for timber increased, and the natural vegetation was replaced by agriculture, at first on the more level heights but later on the steep western slopes as the art of terracing developed about 1000 B.C. The eastern slopes, being in a rain shadow and therefore much drier, were grazing land at the higher levels but changed rapidly to desert in the depths of the Rift Valley. The new farming land reflected the natural cover that had disappeared: forest trees were replaced by olive groves, scrub woodland by vines, and grassland by wheat or barley, the three together providing "wine to gladden the heart of man, oil to make his face shine, and bread to strengthen man's heart" (Ps. 104:15). Although one of these three was often dominant—e.g., olives on the Cenomanian limestone of Ephraim in the central highlands, vines on the drier highlands of Judah further south, and wheat on the Senonian chalk of Manasseh north of Ephraim as well as in the rich Valley of Jezreel—all three were cultivated together throughout the Israelite homeland. In fact, the Israelites never settled permanently in any area where all three were not possible. When foreign nations jeered at the Israelites, asking "Where is their God?"

> Then the Lord became jealous for his land,
>   and had pity on his people.
> The Lord answered and said to his people,
> "Behold, I am sending to you
>   grain, wine, and oil,
>   and you will be satisfied."
>
> (Joel 2:17–19)[3]

Deuteronomy 8:7–9 has a more complete and impressive list:

> The Lord your God is bringing you into a good land, a land of brooks of water, of fountains of springs, flowing forth in valleys and hills, a land of wheat and barley, of vines and fig trees and pomegranates, a land of olive trees and honey, a land in which you will eat bread without scarcity, in which you will lack nothing.

This glowing picture, although altogether accurate in one sense, nevertheless promised too much for years of famine and drought did occur, sometimes even three years in succession without sufficient rainfall (1 Kings 17:1),[4] causing disastrous results. Much of the cultivated land was marginal and very susceptible to fluctuations in rainfall. A succession of good years encouraged farmers to extend their fields well into the desert, but failures of the rain could cast them into total destitution, forcing them to take refuge elsewhere. The neighboring Bedouin, themselves desperate for pasture, had little alternative but to advance on the deserted fields.

The Israelites, in fact, never settled permanently in any area where the wheat, olives, and vines could not be cultivated together and therefore the Syrians said that "their gods are gods of the hills." The only plain they effectively incorporated was the narrow Plain of Jezreel (Esdraelon) where "the grain, the wine, and the oil" were all possible (Hosea 2:22).

In addition to these basic products there were many others. In drier regions wheat was replaced by barley, and the barley at Bethlehem,

---

3. See also Gen. 27:28, 37; Deut. 7:13; 11:14; 12:17; 14:23; 18:4; 28:51; 33:28; 2 Kings 18:32; 2 Chron. 31:5; 32:28; Neh. 5:11; 10:39; 13:5, 12; Ps. 4:7; Isa. 36:17; Lam. 2:12; Hos. 2:5, 8, 22; Joel 1:10; Hag. 1:11; all these indicate the dominance of these three products.

4. "Neither dew nor rain" means woefully insufficient rain. In 1957–60 Jerusalem received less than half its normal supply of rain and it was then quite common to hear people say, "We have had no rain for three years."

mentioned in chapters 2 and 3 of Ruth, was probably grown on the eastern slopes. Garden products such as cucumbers (Isa. 1:8), dill, mint, and cummin (Isa. 28:27; Matt. 23:23) were very common. Fruit trees included almonds (Gen. 43:11),[5] figs (Micah 7:1; Hosea 9:10), and pomegranates (Deut. 8:8; 1 Sam. 14:2; Song of Sol. 4:3, 13; 6:7, 11; 8:2). Dates, particularly valued for their sugar, were grown in the hot Dead Sea area, especially at Jericho.

DOMESTIC AND WILD ANIMALS

> So he lodged there that night, and took from what he had with him a present for brother Esau, two hundred she-goats and twenty he-goats, two hundred ewes and twenty rams, thirty milch camels and their colts, forty cows and ten bulls, twenty she-asses and ten he-asses. (Gen. 32:13-15)

This munificent gift by which Jacob hoped to pacify his brother Esau includes all the domesticated animals of ancient Palestine except dogs and horses. Dogs were very common and valuable as scavengers (Exod. 22:31; 1 Kings 14:11; 22:38; 2 Kings 9:10, 36; Mark 7:27), but for that reason were despised (2 Sam. 3:8; 16:9; Eccles. 9:4; Isa. 56:10; Phil. 3:2). Horses, on the other hand, were a royal possession and bred for warfare (1 Kings 20:25). Chariot warfare was not suited to the often rocky hill country of Israel and therefore horses were thought by many to be characteristic of Egypt and consequently of tyranny (Gen. 15:1; Deut. 17:16). Solomon was the first king of Israel to assemble a large stable (1 Kings 4:26-28; 10:26), and is reported to have acted as a middleman in the trade between Egypt and the northern kingdoms of Syria and Anatolia (1 Kings 10:28-29).

The sheep, goats, donkeys, and camels, on the other hand, were the animals of everyday life, although the list already quoted was more characteristic of the Eastern Plateau and the southern deserts than of the farmland on the Palestinian highlands. Nevertheless, since so many of the towns and villages on the central ridge lay close to the drought-stricken eastern slopes, agriculture was often combined with

---

5. The almond tree is the first fruit tree to blossom in the spring and is therefore in Hebrew challed *shaked*, the "wakeful tree." Hence the play on words in Jer. 1:11-12 between *shaked* and *shoked* ("awake").

the rearing of sheep and goats, sheep being the more valuable but goats the more hardy and suited to desert conditions. Both were valuable as food (Deut. 14:4) and for providing wool or hair for clothing, and both also were reared as sacrificial animals, especially after the Temple was built in Jerusalem. For the ordinary villager and the shopkeeper or craftworker in the city, however, eating meat was probably confined to festive occasions. It would have been too expensive for everyday consumption.

Camels are desert animals and therefore marginal to the Palestinian area.[6] They appear to have been first domesticated in southern Arabia sometime between 3000 and 2500 B.C. and to have penetrated as domestic animals only slowly to the north. Although present evidence suggests that they were known in Syria and Palestine, they must have been exceedingly rare. The "thirty milch camels and their colts" said to have been given to Esau by Jacob is therefore an anachronism.[7] In the two centuries before the accession of King David in about 1000 B.C. domesticated camels were beginning to come into use in Palestine, and as the monarchy developed they must have become increasingly common. Nevertheless, they were always more numerous in the southern desert and on the high Eastern Plateau where there were great herds of them.

THE WILDERNESS AND THE WOODS

> I will make with them a covenant of peace and banish wild beasts from the land, so that they may dwell securely in the wilderness and sleep in the woods. (Ezek. 34:25)

Until the rise of the Hellenistic period after Alexander's victory at Issus in 333 B.C., Palestine and Transjordan were lands of little towns and even smaller villages. What is called a "city" in most translations of the Old Testament was a walled settlement of about ten acres in area, with a correspondingly small population crowded together

---

6. The best book on the subject of camels and their history is Richard W. Bulliet, *The Camel and the Wheel* (Cambridge: Harvard University Press, 1975). I am indebted to this book for much of the information given here.

7. The date of the Patriarchs is now a matter of dispute among scholars, but even if the late date now suggested by some scholars is accepted, the number seems excessive.

within its defenses. Jerusalem became larger when Solomon built the Temple and his palace at the northern end of it, and larger still when King Hezekiah had to provide room for the refugees from Samaria, which had been conquered by the Assyrians in 721 B.C. Even so, it never became larger than about twenty-five acres.

The cultivated land did not extend far from the villages and large areas, especially during the early period and through all the monarchy, must have remained untended with no permanent settlements. These areas were the *midbar* and the *ya'ar*, terms which have been constantly misunderstood by biblical scholars.

Midbar is normally translated "desert," but this is misleading since, although it includes all the true desert and semidesert areas, it also includes much that we today would not call desert at all, e.g., the wide area of poor pastureland immediately east of Bethlehem, the *midbar* in which the youthful David left the sheep when he went down to the encounter with Goliath (1 Sam. 17:28), the same area where the shepherds in the Christmas story kept watch over their flocks (Luke 2:8). A much better translation would be "wilderness," for it is the *wild*, uncultivated land where the villagers and townsfolk find themselves be*wild*ered. The same translation should be used for the Greek *eremos* and *eremeia*. There is a wide expanse of this wild land immediately west and southwest of the Lake of Galilee on the basalt plateau where "Jotham ran away and fled, and went to Beer[8] and dwelt there, for fear of Abimelech his brother" (Judges 9:21), and which may also have been the "wilderness" where Jesus fed the five thousand (Matt. 14:13–21; Mark 6:30–44; Luke 9:10–17).[9]

Ya'ar, normally translated "forest," is the normal word for true forest such as the celebrated forests of Lebanon (1 Kings 7:2; 10:17, 21; 2 Chron. 9:16, 20; Isa. 37:24; 44:14, 23; Zech 11:2), but Ezekiel speaks of "the *ya'ar* of the Negeb" (Ezek. 20:46) on the edge of the desert. Palestine and Transjordan never had majestic forests like those of the Lebanese mountains, but much true forest remained in Old Testament times on the Mount Carmel ridge and on the rainy side of

---

8. Probably al-Bira, 1 1/4 miles (2 km) northwest of Belvoir.

9. John places this miracle in pagan country, on the plateau east of the lake, where according to Matthew and Mark the feeding of the four thousand took place (Matt. 15:32–39; Mark 8:1–10).

the central highland, though in the course of centuries they fell increasingly victim to the woodman's axe, especially after the introduction of iron tools in about 1000 B.C. Even in the New Testament, however, some forests remained, notably in western Upper Galilee, which did not become settled until after the destruction of Jerusalem by the Romans in A.D. 70, and also east of the Jordan in Gilead, where patches of residual forest still exist.

But *ya'ar* also means "tangled bush country," such as we today would call technically "maquis," and the tangle of thorny scrub that takes over when cultivated farmland is deserted, for instance when in time of war refugees flee from their homes. In Hosea 2:12 (Heb. 2:14) God warns the people of the northern kingdom of Israel, "I will lay waste her vines and her fig trees . . . I will make them a *ya'ar*, and the beasts of the field shall devour them." *Ya'ar* and *midbar* indeed often merge into each other, and both frightened the stay-at-home villagers and townspeople who could find in them no clear paths, only trackless wasteland, the home of terrifying wild beasts. These were plentiful and dangerous—lions, wild boar, and crocodiles in the jungle of the River Jordan (Jer. 49:19; 50:17), and leopards and wolves on the Eastern Plateau, as well, of course, as "harts, gazelles, roebucks, and fatted fowl," which were hunted for King Solomon's table (1 Kings 4:23). Moreover, in the long drought of the dry season, refugees in the *midbar*, "greatly distressed and hungry . . . enraged and [cursing] their king and their God" (Isa. 8:21–22), could die of thirst in two days if they lost their way, a danger that still exists for the unwary hiker, even though the wild animals have largely disappeared.

The ancient Israelites, it is true, celebrated the Exodus, the time of their salvation and the giving of the Law in the *midbar*, but they also remembered how terrified they had often been, their desperate lack of food and water, and never did they long to return there. The "desert saints" belong to a very much later period in history.

Mount of Olives. The "Mount" is really a slightly raised part of the plateau. The tower is part of a Russian Orthodox church.

Waterfall near Banias (Caesarea Philippi), one of the sources of the River Jordan.

Petra. The colonnaded street built after the Roman conquest in A.D. 106, and beyond, the towering fortress rock of Umm-el-Biyara.

Caravanserai on the pilgrim road to Mecca, southern Jordan, 1976.

Olive grove in the hill country of Ephraim.

The Desert of Southern Jordan. A broad desert wadi enclosed by high cliffs. The distant mountains reach about 5,000 feet (1,524 m).

River Jordan near Adam. The collapse of the soft marl banks has, on rare occasions, temporarily blocked the flow of the river.

Caesarea Philippi. At Baneas (ancient Paneas) a source of the Jordan flows from the foot of Mount Hermon. Here, Peter confessed that Jesus was the Christ. The niches were dedicated to the god Pan.

The Dissected Desert. Through this majestic scenery of southern Jordan ran the all-important trade route into Arabia and the Yemem.

Jeshimon, the desolate wilderness on the eastern side of Judah.

Shepherd boy with sheep and goats, Wadi Musa, summer 1938.

CHAPTER FOUR

THE REGIONS
OF PALESTINE

Very roughly speaking we may divide Palestine into three parallel north-south zones: the *Western Plains*, the *Central Highlands*, and the *Jordan-Arabah Rift Valley*.

THE WESTERN PLAINS

These begin in the north with the *Plain of Asher*, a very narrow strip of land, usually no more than 5 miles (8 km) wide, between the Central Highlands and the sea. It is really a continuation of the narrow Coast Plain of southern Lebanon and the name "Asher" seems to be more a regional term than a tribal one. The tribe of Asher, in fact, plays an exceedingly small part in Israelite history, although it had the reputation of being rich (Gen. 49:20; Deut. 33:24), for the coast here receives plentiful rain from the winter storms, averaging about 24 inches (600 mm) annually. Unfortunately, it lacks good harbors and is exposed to severe southwest winds. The ancient port of Acco (Judges 1:31), mentioned only once in the Bible, was at Tell el-Fukhkhar now 1 1/4 miles (2 km) inland. The New Testament port of Ptolemais (Acts 21:7), the modern Acre (Acco), was built behind a strong breakwater in the third century B.C.

From the Bay of Acco the rift valley of Esdraelon or Jezreel extends southeastward to Beth-shan and the River Jordan. The central and northwestern sections are drained by the Kishon, which is, however, twice interrupted, once by a narrow little ridge of volcanic basalt between Megiddo and Nazareth and again where the hills of Lower

OLD TESTAMENT PALESTINE

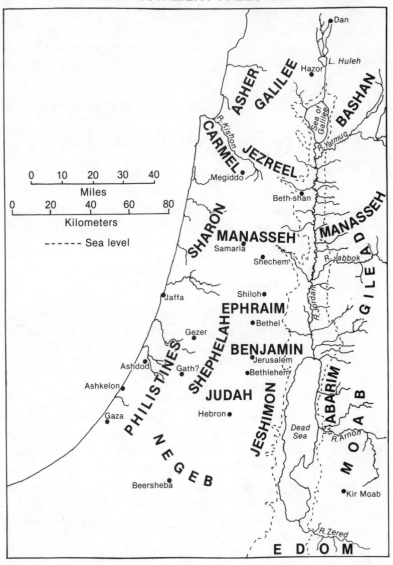

Galilee press close to the slopes of Mount Carmel. The valley is the "rich valley" of Isa. 28:1, with a deep flooring of fertile alluvium, but the hindrances to drainage by the Kishon can cause it to become flooded and impassable. The chariots of Sisera were bogged down in this valley so that he "alighted from his chariot and fled away on foot" (Judges 4:15; 5:20–21), and many years later the prophet Elijah urged King Ahab to hasten his chariot to reach Jezreel before the rain should stop him (1 Kings 18:44). The importance of the town of Megiddo was that it stood where the causeway from Nazareth joins the Megiddo pass, a narrow valley of soft Senonian chalk leading to the coastal Plain of Sharon.

The southeastern section of Esdraelon leads down to Beth-shan, where it drops suddenly into the Jordan rift. It is dominated on the south by the steep slopes of Mount Gilboa, where King Saul's army encamped before his final and fatal battle against the Philistines (1 Sam. 28:4; 31:1–13).

If after exploring the rich valley of Esdraelon we follow the Pass of Megiddo across Mount Carmel southward, we find ourselves in the Plain of Sharon. About 10 miles (16 km) wide, this region is today the scene of rich orange groves and was famous in Israelite times for its luxuriant vegetation (Song of Sol. 2:1; Isa. 33:9; 35:2), but it was in fact almost completely uninhabited. Thickly wooded, it was also very marshy since drainage to the sea is hindered by sand dunes and ridges of a hard, sandy limestone called "kurkah." The international trade route and military highway that led from Aleppo and Damascus, round the Lake of Galilee and through the Pass of Megiddo toward Egypt, here hugged the foot of the Central Highlands as far south as Aphek (modern Rosh ha-'Ayin), the source of the River Yarkon which enters the sea just north of the modern city of Tel Aviv. It is true that there were a few small Iron Age forts along the coast but effective development of this region did not begin until the Hellenistic era in the third century B.C.

The plentiful springs at Aphek made it a strategic site of the utmost importance. Mentioned more than once in ancient Egyptian records, it later became a major Philistine stronghold. In New Testament times this was the fortress of Antipatris, to which the Roman soldiers brought Saint Paul by night (Acts 23:31). About 15 miles (24 km)

47

south of Aphek stood the important strongholds of Gibbethon and Gezer (Tel Malot and Tel Gezer) commanding the Philistine-Israelite frontier in the Valley of Ajalon (Josh. 10:12) and east of them was the Ascent of Beth-horon, the easiest route up into the Central Highlands north of Jerusalem (Josh. 10:10–11; 1 Kings 9:17).

It was at Aphek also that the great north-south road ceased to hug the foot of the mountains and swung southwestward through the territory of the Philistines who had moved into the southern coastal region at about the same time as the Israelites had been occupying the central hill country. They were part of the second wave of "Sea Peoples," against whom Rameses III of Egypt had fought, and apparently it was with Egyptian support that they had occupied southwestern Palestine in about 1150 B.C., though some had settled there earlier.

The coast here is backed up by high sand dunes about 3 miles (4.8 km) in width and the highway runs behind them, its course determined more and more by the necessity of finding water. The Philistine Plain is about 13 miles (20.8 km) wide and characterized by wheat fields in the north and by barley and sheep-rearing in the drier south. Olives will grow close to the coast and date palms near Gaza.

The five major Philistine towns were Ashdod, Ashkelon, and Gaza in the west, and in the east Ekron (Khirbet el-Muqanna, Tel Miqne) and Gath (Tell es-Safi, Tel Zafit). Only Ashkelon was actually on the coast but Ashdod during the later Judean monarchy had a stronghold on the shore at Ashdod-yam. Gaza marks the junction with the desert and the gateway into Egypt. From these five towns, and perhaps especially from Gath since the name became for the Israelites symbolic of the hated Philistines (2 Sam. 1:20; Micah 1:10), the Philistine armies forced their way up into the highlands opposite them, and also northward along the main highway into Esdraelon. In the days of King Saul, when they had iron weapons and the Israelites did not (Josh. 17:16, 18; Judges 1:19; 1 Sam. 13:20),[1] they controlled the important fortress of Beth-shan (1 Sam. 31:10), from which they domi-

---

1. The Israelites were already beginning to use iron in this period but it would seem that they had learned the technique from the Philistines. Not until the time of King David did they acquire the efficiency that enabled them to overcome the Philistine expansion.

nated not only Esdraelon but also the Jordan Valley as far south as the confluence with the River Jabbok.

Between the Philistine Plain and the highlands of Judah is the hill country of the Shephelah, some 27 miles (45 km) long from north to south by 10 miles (16 km) wide. These hills of chalky limestone are not very fertile and were in ancient times covered with rough woodland, but the valleys, such as the Valley of Sorek famous for the exploits of Samson (Judges 13:16), were excellent farming country. Strategically the Shephelah was a buffer zone between the Philistines and the people of Judah, belonging to neither side but fought over by both. On the east it is divided from the highlands by what we may call the "Judean Moat," a long narrow valley of soft Senonian chalk running southward from Aijalon (modern Yalo), a very effective protection for Judah. Many famous armies, from the Philistines to Richard I of England and even later, have taken possession of the Shephelah and yet have failed to conquer Judah.

THE CENTRAL HIGHLANDS

These form four main regions, though each must be subdivided. From north to south they are *Galilee*, north of the Esdraelon Valley; *Manasseh and Ephraim*, with an extension in Mount Carmel; *Judah*, centered on Jerusalem and Hebron; the *Negeb*, south of Beersheba.

Galilee is divided by the tremendous west-east Shaghur fault line into Upper Galilee in the north, everywhere over 2000 feet and sometimes exceeding 3000 feet (roughly 600 m and 900 m), and Lower Galilee to the south, which is nowhere above 2000 feet (600 m) and usually very much less. Both Upper and Lower Galilee are also divided into a broader and usually higher western section, which gets the full effect of the rain-bearing winds in winter, and a narrower, somewhat lower, and decidedly drier, eastern section.

Upper Galilee stands aloof from the biblical story, for throughout the entire period the high western mountain slopes were clothed with thick forest and seem to have been largely uninhabited. The eastern section is less precipitous and a road, at any rate in Roman times, led northward into what is now Lebanon. This is the only part of Upper Galilee mentioned by the Jewish historian Josephus, and the sole biblical reference to it is of the "waters of Merom," probably the Nahal 'Ammud (Wadi Leimun) flowing south toward the Lake of Galilee. Here the kings of Canaan are said to have encamped against Joshua (Josh. 11:5).

Lower Galilee in the "Galilee" of the New Testament, but apart from those beside the lake only three places are in fact mentioned: Nazareth, where Jesus spent his childhood, Nain on the slopes of Mt. Moreh where he raised the widow's son (Luke 7:11), and Cana where he turned the water into wine.[2] In his day Nazareth, which is now the chief town, was no more than a village, and the most important center was Sepphoris (modern Saffuriyeh), about 4 miles (6.4 km) to the northwest on the main road from the port of Ptolemais to the lakeside town of Tiberias.

This broad western section consists of a number of small basins divided by low hills. The drainage from the basins is sometimes hindered by narrow exits and winter flooding is possible, but the fertile alluvium can produce rich harvests of wheat. The hills in Old Testament times supported sheep and goats but were probably still largely wooded. In principle this was the tribal area of Zebulun but they seem in fact to have overflowed into the much richer plain of Esdraelon.

The narrower eastern section, overlooking the Lake of Galilee, is in general rough basalt country, especially in the south. Known to the Arabs as Bilād al-Hawa, the windy lands, it remained, even in New Testament times, essentially "wilderness" with very little settlement.

South of the lowland corridor of Esdraelon the central mountains continue again in the tribal territories of Manasseh and Ephraim. Manasseh in the north is structurally a basin although the hard Eocene limestone in the center forms the twin mountains of Ebal and Gerizim enclosing the town of Shechem (near modern Nablus) between them. The basin structure meant that the soft Senonian chalk valleys led into the heart of Manasseh instead of forming a defensive moat such as protected Judah. In order to survive, therefore, Manasseh struggled to dominate the surrounding tribes and especially to conquer the rich

---

2. Despite tradition, which places it at Kafr Kanna on the road to Tiberias, the correct site of Cana is probably Khirbet Qana 10 miles (about 14 km) north of Nazareth.

Esdraelon Valley, which also gave it control of part of the great north-south trade route from Damascus to Egypt. But such control, even though it brought great wealth, was dangerous, and the northern kingdom, with its capital at Samaria, fell to the Assyrians in 711 B.C.

The dome of hard Cenomanian limestone is much easier to describe than the more complicated basin of Manasseh. The north-south road climbs up onto the highland from the fertile basin of Lebonah (modern Lubban),[3] and follows the summit in a more or less southerly direction through Bethel on the southern border of Ephraim toward Jerusalem. Access to Ephraim from both west and east, though not impossible, is difficult since the approaches are steep and rocky and the western slopes were, in ancient times, thickly forested. Clearing of the forests made room for almost continuous olive groves, "the finest produce of the ancient mountains, and the abundance of the everlasting hills" (Deut. 33:15). East of the highway, when the descent into the Rift Valley begins, the olive orchards give place to rough grazing for sheep and goats, and ultimately to semidesert.

The crags and forests provided a valuable stronghold in the perilous days of the Judges and Ephraim was then a dominant tribe, but the lack of easy communications meant that with the creation of the northern kingdom of Israel power passed into the hands of the more central and much-richer tribe of Manasseh. Only two places in Ephraim remained important in history, both of them ancient sanctuaries: Shiloh in the north and Bethel in the south. The Ark was kept at Shiloh until its capture by the Philistines (1 Sam. 5:11) and the site remained sacred for long afterward (1 Kings 14:1ff.). Bethel was already sacred in the time of the Patriarchs (Gen. 12:8; 13:3; 28:10–17), and Jeroboam I of Israel made it into one of the major border sanctuaries, "a temple of the kingdom" (Amos 7:13).

The road southward from Bethel descends about 400 feet (about 120 m) to the Saddle of Benjamin, the smallest of the Israelite tribes but by no means the least important. Communication was easy down both the western and eastern slopes—to the west by way of the Ascent of

---

3. Lebonah was "a day's journey" from Jerusalem and therefore the place where Jesus' parents discovered that he was not among the caravan of Passover pilgrims (Luke 2:41ff.).

Beth-horon (Josh. 10:10–11; 1 Sam. 13:18; 1 Kings 9:17) and to the east down the Wadi Qilt to Jericho. All this coming and going across Benjamin certainly led to war but it also fostered trade and with it the growth of sanctuaries, places of assembly to which people came from far and near, such as Bethel, Ramah, Mizpah, and Gibeon (Judges 4:5; 20:1ff.; 1 Sam. 2:11; 10:17; 1 Kings 3:4; 1 Chron. 16:37–42).[4]

Jerusalem stands on the border between Benjamin and Judah and before its capture by King David belonged to neither. It probably owed its freedom to a very long history of sanctity because, as history has shown, it is by no means impregnable. After its establishment as the royal capital it became the administrative center and the national sanctuary.[5]

Judah resembles Ephraim in that it is a mountainous stronghold, difficult to penetrate from both east and west, but the rainfall decreases steadily as one proceeds south. Olive groves become markedly fewer, although they do not disappear, and their place is taken by vineyards, for the deep roots of the vine can resist the drought. There are four clearly defined regions mentioned in the Book of Joshua: the *Hill Country or Mountain, the Lowland, the Wilderness, and the South* (Josh. 15:21, 33, 48, 61). The Lowland is the Shephelah already discussed, and the Wilderness is the dread *Jeshimon* (Num. 21:20; 23:28; 1 Sam. 23:24; 26:1; etc.), where the sudden descent to the Dead Sea, 4000 feet (1200 m) below, and the sharp decrease in rainfall combine to make this a desolate and dangerous region, cleft by deep, precipitous gorges. It was here that David fled to escape from Saul (1 Sam. 23:15).

The essential Judah was the Mountain with its center at Hebron, the traditional burial place of the Patriarchs and still today a place of

---

4. Centers of pilgrimage are very often places where roads meet and traders come together, e.g., Mecca in Arabia, Chartres in France, Kiev in Russia. The sanctity and the commerce feed each other, for the merchants need assured peace and the pilgrims need to sell goods in order to pay for their journey. This does not mean that the sanctity is not authentic, merely that it goes hand in hand with trade.

5. Still today it remains profoundly sacred to the adherents of three religions: Judaism, Christianity, and Islam. It is a serious mistake to imagine, as many Westerners do, that Jerusalem is somehow less sacred to Muslims because they have Mecca. For them there are three cities of intense sanctity: Mecca the Blessed, Medina the Radiant, the Jerusalem the Holy. Arabs are in fact the only people who call Jerusalem "the Holy" (al-Quds) in ordinary, everyday speech.

great sanctity to both Muslims and Jews. The highway to the south ran along the ridge but in general the villages and small towns (there were no large ones) stood to one side, close to the springs. Bethlehem in the north, now a sizable town and almost contiguous with Jerusalem, was throughout biblical times no more than a village on the springline overlooking the Jeshimon.

The Mountain comes to an end just north of Beersheba, the southern frontier town of Judah, and another sacred city (Amos 5:5; 8:14). Here begins the southern descent through which the mountain ridge continues at a much lower level toward Sinai. Known today as the Negev, it was settled only intermittently and for long periods was given over entirely to the Bedouin. In the New Testament period, however, and for some centuries afterward, a handful of towns were built here by the Nabateans and Romans, e.g., Kurnub, Oboda, Nessana, and Subeita, to maintain the rich trade routes from Arabia to the Mediterranean.

The modern use of the word "Negev" to cover the entire southern region is unfortunately somewhat misleading, because the Old Testament "Negeb," the Southland of Josh. 15:21 and elsewhere, denoted a very much smaller area. This was a broad sickle of land extending round the southern and southwestern foothills of Judah, where barley cultivation and sheep-rearing were still possible, and where there were sufficient springs to enable the building of a line of fortresses to protect the approaches to the Judean highlands.

THE JORDAN-ARABAH RIFT VALLEY

A sudden steep descent of about 400 feet (125 m) divides the higher northern section of the great Central Rift Valley from the lower southern section. This was not only a persistent frontier zone, as it still is today, but a region of profound sanctity, with thick mysterious forests and rivers gushing out of the foot of the towering snow-clad Mount Hermon. Every place mentioned in the Bible was a notable sanctuary: Abel-beth-Maacah, where men came to consult the oracle (2 Sam. 20:18); Dan, with its great temple built by Jeroboam I (1 Kings 12:29; 2 Kings 10:29; Amos 8:14); and Caesarea Philippi, where King Herod built a temple dedicated to Emperor Augustus, and where Jesus asked his disciples the critical question, "Who do you say that I am?" (Mark 8:29).[6]

South of these ancient sanctuaries is the Huleh Basin, about 14 miles long and 5 miles wide (22 km x 8 km). Now drained, it was in biblical times a tangled and marshy jungle ending in the shallow Lake Huleh. The only road from the north hugs the foot of the Galilee Mountains. Immediately south of the lake one branch of the great north-south highway from Damascus to Egypt crossed the Jordan at the charmingly named "Bridge of Jacob's Daughters"[7] to join the road from Dan just south of the great Bronze Age city of Hazor, "formerly the head of all those kingdoms" (Josh. 11:10), destroyed by Joshua but rebuilt later by Solomon (1 Kings 9:15) and strengthened by King Ahab.

South of Lake Huleh the Jordan tumbles down to the Lake of Galilee through a precipitous gorge, sometimes 1000 feet (300 m) deep, carved out of a great outflow of basalt that blocks the valley. The heart-shaped lake is no more than 12 miles long by 7 miles wide (18 km x 12 km) and in the Old Testament appears only as a boundary (Num. 34:11; Josh. 11:2). In New Testament times, however, it was the scene of vigorous commercial life, exporting to Rome fish from the lake and wheat from the plateau of Bashan on the east. The chief town, then as now, was Tiberias, famous for its hot springs but playing no part in the Gospels. Capernaum, the center of Jesus' activity, is in the north-west. The ruins of its fine synagogue belong to a much later period but may well stand on the same site as the synagogue in which he taught. South of Capernaum is the narrow Plain of Gennesaret from which the Damascus-Egypt highway climbs into the hills of Lower Galilee.

From the Lake of Galilee, 695 feet (212 m) below sea level, to the Dead Sea is no more than 65 miles (105 km) but the meandering River Jordan covers 200 miles (320 km) in its descent. Halfway to the Dead Sea the mountains on both sides press in to pinch the valley in a narrow "waist." The Rift Valley is everywhere in a rain shadow, but this "waist" marks an important divide between the wetter north and the

---

6. Caesarea Philippi was the name given when Philip became ruler of southern Syria (Luke 3:1), but the ancient name was Paneas, preserved in the modern Arabic name, Banias. The place was sacred to the forest god Pan, and niches carved in the rock to hold images of him may still be seen today.

7. The name comes from the "Daughters of St. James" who had a convent here in the Crusading period. It has nothing to do with the Jacob of the Old Testament.

drought-bitten south. The average annual rainfall at Dan in the far north is 24 inches (600 mm), at Tiberias 16 inches (400 mm), and at Jericho no more than 5 inches (125 mm). The "waist" separates the cultivable land from the desert. Although some important western streams do flow into the Jordan, by far the greater amount of water comes from the steep plateau slopes to the east, which face the rain-bearing winds. Immediately south of the "waist" the plentiful River Jabbok joins the Jordan from the east, and the much-smaller Fari'a from the west. Close to the confluence is the important ford of Adam, where the waters were dammed up in the days of Joshua (Josh. 3:16).[8]

The Jordan south of the "waist" meanders in a deep trough, filled with an almost impenetrable mass of tamarisks and other shrubs, the "pride of Jordan" (Jer. 12:5; Zech. 11:3), the haunt of many savage beasts (as late as World War II there were still wild boar here). On each side of this jungle are the altogether barren badlands known to-day as the Qattara, and beyond them a gently sloping barren plain which could be cultivated only close to the foot of the mountains, as for instance at Jericho, a settlement with ten thousand years of history.

The Dead Sea is almost exactly halfway from Dan to Elath on the Red Sea. Its surface is 1295 feet (395 m) below sea level and the greatest depth reaches twice that figure. The most saline body of water in the world, with a 25-percent mineral content, it is entirely without life, and the narrow shores are pitiless desert with an average annual rainfall of only 2 inches (50 mm). But occasionally they can be drenched by heavy storms and on these rare occasions the desert bursts into colorful life.

The western slopes are especially desolate but there are two impor-tant springs: at 'Ain Feshka in the north, close to Qumran where the first Dead Sea Scrolls were discovered, and at Engedi in the center. In the extreme southwest is the great salt dome of Har Sdom, which is prob-ably related to the strange story of Lot's wife (Gen. 19:26). A road is possible along the narrow western shore, but on the east towering precipices rise straight out of water, interrupted only by the gorges of

---

8. The collapse of the banks at this point and consequent blockage of the river hap-pened once during the Crusades and once again early in this century. Whether it oc-curred at any other time we do not know.

the Zerqa Ma'in and the River Arnon. Only in the southeast, behind the peninsula of the Lisan, is there a narrow plain where winter crops are grown. Overlooking the Lisan on the western side of the Dead Sea is the towering rock of Masada where Herod the Great built an impressive palace, but where Sodom and Gomorrah stood nobody knows, nor are there any trustworthy clues. The most reasonable suggestion is that they may have vanished beneath the shallow southern basin of the sea.

The long stretch between the Dead Sea and the Red Sea is today normally called the Arabah, although properly speaking, both in the Bible and in modern Arabic, the word applies to the whole valley south of the Lake of Galilee. Here we will keep the common usage. About 100 miles (160 km) long, it rises gently from the Dead Sea to 655 feet (200 km) above sea level in the center and then descends gradually to the Gulf of Aqabah.

Immediately south of the Dead Sea is the Sebkha, a desolate and salty wasteland, which some hundred years ago was covered by the Dead Sea. But south of this dreary wilderness the Arabah widens out. On the west is the broad Biq'at Zin (Wadi Murra), the easiest and most important route across the Negev to the Mediterranean, and on the east is the Punon Embayment, which will be discussed in the next chapter. South of the central divide the Arabah narrows to no more than 6 miles (10 km) in width with steep cliffs on both sides until finally the Red Sea is reached.

The importance of the Arabah for the kings of Judah was (1) the presence of copper, notably at Punon (Feinan) on the eastern side, and (2) access to the Red Sea trade, which was achieved by Solomon (1 Kings 9:26), by Jehoshaphat (1 Kings 22:47), and for the last time by Uzziah (2 Kings 14:22). There are sufficient springs to make travel relatively easy, and before it was destroyed by overgrazing, a considerable amount of rough scrub vegetation, but there was always the danger of tempestuous winds, flash floods in winter, and fierce attacks by the jealous Edomites, anxious to preserve a trading monopoly.

At the center of the Red Sea shore there is a ruined fortress, apparently built by Solomon, and probably to be identified with Eziongeber (1 Kings 9:26). Some metal working was done here, but it seems to have been mainly a fortified caravanserai. The chief port must always have been the oasis of Aqabah at the foot of the Edomite mountains.

CHAPTER FIVE

EAST OF
THE JORDAN

East of the tremendous trough of the Jordan-Arabah Rift Valley is the vast Arabian plateau, for the most part cruel desert, the home in olden times of hardy, fiercely independent, Bedouin. We are here concerned only with the northwestern edge of it, extending from Damascus in Syria to the Red Sea at Aqabah, but Arabia looming behind must never be forgotten. Mysterious and frightening the desert doubtless was to the settled farmer, but out of it came the lumbering caravans, "perfumed with myrrh and frankincense, with all the fragrant powders of the merchant" (Song of Sol. 3:6), and "wise men from the East," bringing with them "gifts, gold and frankincense and myrrh" (Matt. 2:1, 11). In times of ruthless foreign invasion, such as that of the Assyrians in the eighth century B.C., villagers and townspeople fled from Palestine to Arabia:

> In the thickets in Arabia you will lodge,
>   O caravans of Dedanites.
> To the thirsty bring water,
>   meet the fugitive with bread,
>   O inhabitants of the land of Tema.
> For they have fled from the swords,
>   from the drawn sword,
> from the bent bow
>   and from the press of battle.
>   (Isa. 21:13–15)

The plateau edge is cleft by deep canyons, of which the four major ones are (1) the Yarmuq in the north, today dividing modern Syria

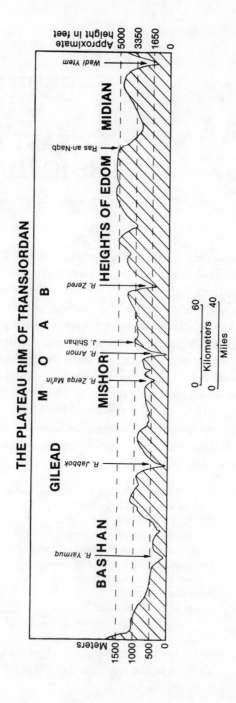

THE PLATEAU RIM OF TRANSJORDAN

from Jordan; (2) the Jabbok (modern Zerqa) farther south; (3) the Arnon (Mojjib), with its tributary the Wala, entering the Dead Sea north of the Lisan peninsula; and finally (4) the Zered (Wadi Hesa) flowing into the southern end of the Dead Sea. All four are obvious strategic frontiers and are sometimes so described in the Old Testament (Num. 21:13; Deut. 3:16; Judges 11:28), but only the Zered in the south separates two different natural regions from each other. Elsewhere a common way of life spreads across both sides of the canyon. We may divide these different ways of life into the Farmer of Bashan in the north, the Highlander of Gilead, the Shepherd of Ammon and Moab, and in the far south the Trader of Edom. Farther out to the east lived the Warrior of Mount Bashan (modern Jebel Druze), and the Nomad of the Desert.

THE PLATEAU OF BASHAN, THE LAND OF THE FARMER

This lies directly east of the Lake of Galilee and south of Mount Hermon, and extends southward across the Yarmuq canyon to the foothills of Gilead. The western edge of the plateau, known to us today as the Golan Heights, is formed of lines of volcanic cones, called *tulūl*,[1] and was in Old Testament times the tribal territory of Geshur and Maacah (Josh. 13:11-13; 2 Sam. 13:37-38; 1 Chron. 19:6-7). East of this was the plateau of Bashan, well watered and with a covering of fertile volcanic soil. It was famous for its wheatfields and for its abundant pasture, and Ezekiel in the Gog and Magog oracle speaks of "rams, of lambs, and of goats, of bulls, all of them fatlings of Bashan" (Ezek. 39:18).[2] These animals probably belonged more to the *tulūl* than to the level plateau, which would be mainly given over to wheat. *Tulūl*, although concentrated in the west, are found all over the Bashan plateau.

The Old Testament twice mentions "the region of Argob" as being "in Bashan" with "sixty cities . . . fortified with high walls, gates, and

---

1. *Tulūl* is the plural of *tell*, meaning a rounded hill. In Western terminology it is used for archaeological mounds, e.g., *Tel as-Sultan* or *Tulūl adh-Dhabab*, but in Arabic it may be used also for any kind of rounded hill, large or small.

2. See also Deut. 32:14; Ps. 22:12.

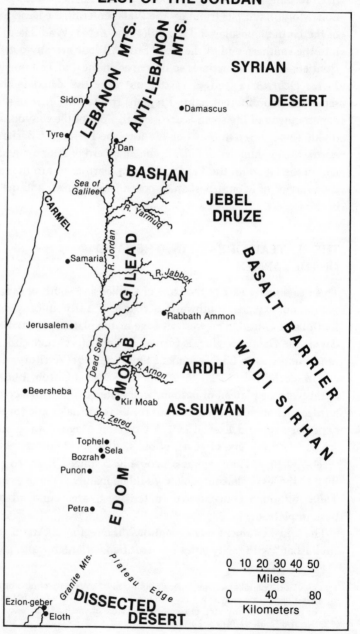

bars, besides very many unwalled villages" (Deut. 3:4-5; 1 Kings 4:13), and as having been in pre-Israelite days "the kingdom of Og," a somewhat mysterious figure who lived at Edrei, the modern Dera'a, and at 'Ashtaroth (Tell 'Ashtarah), and who controlled the entire region (Num. 21:33; Deut. 1:4; 3:1, 10; Josh. 12:4; 13:12, 31). The high walls and strongly defended gates were very necessary, for the wide-open plateau has no natural defenses.

Further to the east is the "many-peaked mountain of Bashan" (Ps. 68:15), a black, rocky, and volcanic mass, reaching 5,789 feet (1,764 m) at its highest point. The western slopes receive plentiful rain and heavy snow in winter (Ps. 68:14), but the eastern slopes grade off rapidly into the desert. The home throughout history of fiercely independent people, who must always wrestle with the brutal basalt to produce their food, mainly wheat, barley, vines, and vegetables, it was in ancient times famous for its dense forests. Today these have been replaced by thick and tangled maquis, but then trees were many and wood plentiful. Nevertheless the hard rock gives little room for roots to spread and the trees can never have been majestic, nor the lumber suitable for building houses, for even roofs, doors, and window frames were often made of the dark and gloomy basalt. That the prophets should compare these forests to the majestic cedars of Lebanon (Isa. 2:13; Ezek. 27:5-6) is evidence that they knew this region only by hearsay. Only one town on this mountain is ever mentioned in the Old Testament—Salecah (modern Salkhad), and always as the most remote settlement in the east (Deut. 3:10; Josh. 12:5; 13:11; 1 Chron. 5:11).

GILEAD, THE LAND OF THE HIGHLANDER

This great dome of Cenomanian limestone is a continuation at a higher level of the Judean highlands to the southwest. It is cleft in two by the canyon of the Jabbok (modern Zerqa), which rises at Rabbah of the Ammonites (modern Amman) and flows at first northeastward to Zerqa, and then curves round to enter the Rift Valley near the ancient Penuel (Tulūl adh-Dhahab), where for a time Jeroboam I seems to have had his capital (1 Kings 12:25), and where much earlier Jacob is said to have wrestled with the angel (Gen. 32:22-30). This deep canyon certainly formed an administrative boundary, and before the Israelite occupation Sihon ruled the southern half and Og the northern (Josh. 12:2, 5). After their defeat the southern district was allotted to the tribes of Gad and Reuben and the northern district to half the tribe of Manasseh.

Gilead is the only part of the Transjordan plateau where wheat, grapes, and olives can all be grown together and is therefore the only region where the traditional Israelite way of life was possible and where they settled. In fact, however, only the northern section with its greater height and thicker forests[3] remained in their hands. The southern section is more open to penetration by people from the east and south, the Ammonites (Amos 1:13) and the Moabites, and so the tribes of Reuben and Gad gradually disappeared from history, although we do know from the Moabite Stone[4] that in about 850 B.C. there was still an Israelite sanctuary at Mt. Nebo, from which Moses had surveyed the promised land and where, according to tradition, he died (Deut. 34:1-6).

Mt. Nebo overlooks the *Abarim*, the "regions beyond," often called *Harei ha-Abarim*, the "mountains of the further regions" (Num. 27:12; 33:45-48; Deut. 32:49). The name clearly reflects the view of them from the distant Judean highlands to the west, for in fact they are not mountains at all. They are, it is true, structurally the narrow tail end of mountainous Gilead as it sinks into the Dead Sea, but they are everywhere lower than the plateau, whose inhabitants peer down into them from above. It would be much more accurate to call them "scarplands."

The Abarim were evidently settled by Israelites and perched within them, almost due west of Amman, is 'Iraq al-Amir ("Cave of the Prince") where stand today the ruins of a Hellenistic palace, Qasr al-'Abd ("Castle of the Servant," i.e., the governor, the servant of the king). It was the home of the Tobiad family, of whom an earlier "Tobiah the Servant" had hindered the work of Nehemiah after the

---

3. These forests were almost as famous as those of Lebanon (Jer. 22:6; Zech. 10:10), and still today there are areas of woodland, notably the Dibbin Forest south of Ajlun.

4. Discovered in 1868 and now in the Louvre, the Moabite Stone records the victory of King Mesha of Moab over the Israelite forces and the reconquest of the territory north of the Arnon gorge.

return from the Babylonian Exile (Neh. 2:10, 19; 4:3, 7; 6:1ff.; 13:4ff.).

MOAB AND AMMON, THE LAND OF THE SHEPHERD

The broad and relatively level plateau of Moab east of the Dead Sea is much easier to describe. It is divided into two parts by the deep, impressive canyon of the Arnon (modern Mojjib) and its tributary the Hesa. To the north is the *Mishor*, or tableland, where Reuben tarried "among the sheepfolds, to hear the piping for the flocks" (Judges 5:16). By the time of the great prophets in the eighth and seventh centuries it had become, however, firmly Moabite (Isa. 15:4; 16:8–9; Jer. 48:2ff.).

The true heartland of Moab lay to the south between the strong defenses of the Arnon and the Zered canyons. Here the land rises steadily from about 2300 to 3300 feet (about 700–1000 m) and the wheat farming, which was still of great importance north of the Arnon, gives place to pasture. Sheep were everywhere the mainstay of Moabite life:

> Now Mesha king of Moab was a sheep breeder; and he had to deliver annually to the king of Israel a hundred thousand lambs, and the wool of a hundred thousand rams. But when Ahab died, the king of Moab rebelled against the king of Israel. (2 Kings 3:4–5)

It is this revolt and its results that are recounted, from different points of view, on the Moabite Stone and in 2 Kings 3.

The Moabite capital was Kir-hareseth, the modern Kerak.[5] Today crowned by the ruins of a gigantic Crusader's castle, it commands the deep and narrow valley[6] that gives access to the Dead Sea and the narrow, but fertile, plain south of the Lisan peninsula.

The territory of Ammon north of Moab and east of Gilead is difficult to define. Certainly it was centered on Rabboth Ammon, the

---

5. Mesha, however, seems to have had his capital at Dibon (Dhiban), a few miles north of the Arnon.
6. Perhaps the "descent of Horonaim" (Jer. 48:5), but we cannot be sure.

"city of waters" (2 Sam. 12:27), where the great citadel dominates the powerful springs at the head of the River Jabbok and the fertile valley as far as Zerqa 12 1/2 miles (20 km) to the northeast, but its outer limits are very ill-defined, both physically and climatically. Situated on the lee side of the Gilead Mountains, it suffers from being in a rain shadow. Rabboth Ammon (modern Amman) is plentifully supplied by the strong springs of the River Jabbok which were captured for David by Joab (2 Sam. 12:27). In an average year it receives about 12 inches (300 mm) of rain, with 20 inches (500 mm) in a good year, such as 1966–67, but only 4 inches (100 mm) in a bad year, e.g., 1959–60.[7] The Jabbok valley is rich and fertile but Zerqa, only five miles northeast, has about half Amman's rainfall and stands on the edge of the desert. The temptation, therefore, for the Ammonites to "enlarge their border" by pressing up into the better-watered highlands of Gilead was very strong (Amos 1:13).

THE HEIGHTS OF EDOM, THE LAND OF THE TRADER

South of the deep gorge of the Zered (Wadi Hesa) the traveler is immediately aware of a difference in the landscape, for the edge of the plateau has been tilted upward into a great limestone ridge, more than 5,000 feet (1,524 m) above sea level. On the west this descends to the Rift Valley in two broad sandstone steps, eroded by the winter storms into precipitous ridges and valleys, the home until quite recently of wolves, leopards, and other wild animals. On the east the ridge slopes down steeply but smoothly toward the high Arabian plateau. The great height of the westward-facing wall has meant that the ridge receives a fair amount of winter rain,[8] sufficient indeed to clothe it in the past with good woodland—"forest" would perhaps be too strong a

---

7. For these, and all other, climate figures for Transjordan I am indebted to the excellent *National Atlas of Jordan, Part I: Climate and Agroclimatology* (Amman: Jordan National Geographic Center, 1984).

8. About 8 inches (200 mm) annually, though this can vary greatly and decreases toward the south. Rainfall figures for Edom are still somewhat tentative because records have not been kept for a sufficiently long time, and recording stations are at present few.

term. Much of the precipitation comes in the form of snow and winter storms can be savage, even lethal at times.

The ridge is interrupted about 10 miles (16 km) south of the Zered canyon by the Feinan (or Punon) Embayment, a sudden gash caused by two fault lines branching out from Feinan (the Punon of Num. 33:42–43) in the Rift Valley. Feinan may well have been the place where Moses raised the bronze serpent in the wilderness (Num. 21:4–9). Recent work at the site has revealed that copper was mined here on a large scale continuously from the Bronze Age to the Roman period,[9] and it now seems highly probable that this is the true position of "King Solomon's mines."

The Edomite ridge has room for no more than a single line of towns and villages following the line of springs that break out on the western slopes of the ridge just below the summit. The majority of these are north of the embayment, the most wealthy being Tophel (Deut. 1:1), modern Tafileh, with no less than eight strong springs and rich olive groves. The strategic center, however, was Bozrah (Isa. 34:6; 63:1; Jer. 49:13, 22; Amos 1:12; Micah 2:12), modern Buseirah, perched on an isolated spur of highland from which it could dominate both the north-south road and the Wadi Dana, leading down to the rich copper mines at Punon.

South of the embayment the biblical records mention no sites and modern archaelogical research has at present little information to give us. It may be, though we cannot be sure, that this southern region had fewer permanent settlements. The great Nabatean city of Petra with its famous rock-cut tombs and temples belongs to the Hellenistic and Roman periods, i.e., after 330 B.C. Nevertheless, settlement in the region and exchange of products over vast distances can be traced back to about 7000 B.C.

THE DISSECTED DESERT

About 20 miles (32 km) south of Petra the great plateau suddenly comes to an end and the precipitous edge of it curves away to the southeast. Instantly we are in a quite-different environment, an arid

---

9. Dr. David McCreery, from a personal communication.

network of narrow valleys between gigantic red sandstone cliffs and divided from the Arabah by a hard and towering granite ridge reaching over 5,000 feet (1,524 m) in places. The sandstone cliffs of the interior are no less majestic and those which enclose the famous Wadi Ram reach 5,740 feet (1,750 m) in height, towering 2,200 feet (670 m) above the valley floor. The great height of these mountains means that they receive a certain amount of winter rain or snow although they are so far south, and consequently there are occasional wells or springs at their foot.

The presence of this water in the desert is of the utmost importance because along these corridors lay one of the major ancient trade routes, the "incense road" from southern Arabia to Damascus and the other great mercantile cities of the north, known in the Transjordan section as the "King's Highway."[10] This road climbs up onto the high plateau at Ras an-Naqb and then follows the plateau edge past the Moabite fortress of Kir-hareseth (Kerak) northward until it divides, one branch continuing boldly up into the Gilead Mountains and directly into Bashan, while the other swings round the foot of the mountains past Rabboth Ammon (Amman). At the southern end, in the dissected desert region, a branch of the road leads down through the narrow Wadi Ytem to the oasis port of Aqabah, the ancient Elath.[11] This valley is subject in winter to disastrous flash floods tumbling down enormous boulders that may undermine even modern engineering. The importance of this so-called King's Highway, which connects all the major settlements of Moab and Edom, is made abundantly clear by the long line of Iron Age forts that protect it on the eastern side.

---

10. Num. 20:17. There is today, however, considerable doubt whether this was an official name or whether it was merely a general term for an important road. There do not appear to have been "kings" in Transjordan in the time of the Exodus.

11. The identification of Elath with Tell el-Kheleifeh in the center of the Rift Valley, common in many biblical atlases, must almost certainly be rejected. Tell el-Kheleifeh, which may be Ezion-geber, is an isolated desert fortress and anchorage close to it would expose boats to the tempestuous winds which sweep along the Rift Valley, or the savage northeasters that may pour down from the mountains of Midian (1 Kings 22:48). Aqabah, on the other hand, is a rich oasis where thickly clustered date palms would help to break the force of the storms. Unfortunately, the rapid modern development of the port and resort city at Aqabah has rendered any major archaeological exploration impossible. For an account of the storms see J. R. Wellsted, *Travels in Arabia* (Graz, Austria: Akademische Druck- und Verlagsanstalt, 1978), 2:134–41.

THE PLATEAU DESERT

On a modern map of the Levant one may trace the line of the "Hejaz Railroad" running southward from Damascus through Amman to Ma'an, with today a major highway beside it. This may be said to mark the western edge of the plateau desert. It had always been a vital route for the lumbering merchant caravans going to and from southern Arabia, and with the rise of Islam it became one of the great pilgrim roads leading to Medina and Mecca.[12] East of the railroad is a more or less level but arid plateau. Wells are few and widely scattered, the two most important being in the south, Bayir and al-Jafr. The whole eastern section, sloping down toward the Wadi Sirhan, is the Ardh as-Suwān, covered in every direction by sharp nodules of dark flint with not a blade of grass in sight. The flint is apt to cut the soft feet of the camels and so this region was avoided as much as possible by the desert traveler.

The Wadi Sirhan is a prolonged depression extending southeastward from the oasis of Azraq for about 175 miles (280 km). It is about 55 miles (90 km) wide and on the far side stands a stark, forbidding barrier of hard black basalt, sometimes as much as 60 miles (96 km) wide and towering about 750 feet (225 m), or often very much more, above the Wadi floor. It can be crossed in places, but only with great difficulty, and the caravans steadfastly avoided it. Azraq at its head, where the basalt outflows block the Wadi also from the north, has an excellent water supply from a number of powerful springs, and an abundant animal life.[13] In the New Testament period the Nabatean merchants at Petra brought the Wadi Sirhan under their control, and indeed at one time extended their influence as far as Damascus, so as to circumvent the expanding power and authority of imperial Rome. Finally, however, Rome proved the stronger and Nabatean rule came to an end in A.D. 106.

---

12. Only few, however, use it for the pilgrimage today since other forms of transport are easier. The railroad at one time went as far as Medina, and the disused track still exists. The modern road and railroad turn southeastward, the road joining the "King's Highway" and then to Aqabah, and the railroad going into the Wadi Hasma section of the Dissected Desert, where important experiments in desert farming are under way.

13. In the years after World War II excessive hunting seriously reduced the wildlife. The Jordanian government, however, has now declared the oasis and immediately surrounding region a national park and game reserve.

CHAPTER SIX

NEW TESTAMENT PALESTINE

THE HISTORICAL BACKGROUND

In the two centuries following the return of the Jewish exiles from Babylon their territory around Jerusalem and Hebron was only a very tiny part of the vast Persian Empire, which lasted for over two hundred years from 539 B.C until Alexander's victory in 333 B.C.[1] He died only ten years later, in 323, but because of his overwhelming triumphs Greek culture thereafter dominated the Middle East.

After his death his empire was broken up and Palestine fell victim once again to the ancient rivalry between Egypt and Mesopotamia. For the first twenty-two years the country was shuttled back and forth between the Ptolemies in Egypt and the Seleucid rulers in Mesopotamia, and then in the succeeding two centuries it remained under the domination of Egypt. However, in 198 B.C. it passed into the hands of the Seleucids, who had their capital first at Ctesiphon, close to modern Baghdad, but subsequently at Antioch in southern Turkey just north of the present Syrian frontier. The Seleucid rulers, and notably the insanely cruel Antiochus IV (175–164 B.C.), tried to bring order to their widespread but unruly dominions by imposing upon

---

1. Issus, not far from Antioch in southern Turkey, was the critical victory that enabled Alexander to break through into the Fertile Crescent. He first conquered all the Levant and Egypt and then overcame Mesopotamia, Persia, part of southern Russia, Afghanistan, and what is now Pakistan as far as the River Indus.

them a common Hellenistic way of life, even going so far as to desecrate the Temple in Jerusalem in an effort to eradicate the Jewish religion. A very large number of the Jewish people in Palestine had been greatly attracted by Greek culture, but this scandalous act was altogether unacceptable and brought about the Maccabean revolt, recorded in the First Book of the Maccabees.[2] It began in December 168 B.C., and exactly three years later, in December 165, the Temple was recaptured by Judas Maccabeus and the Jewish worship restored. This has been celebrated ever since by Jews throughout the world in the Festival of Hanukkah.

The rebellion, however, was by no means at an end, and fighting continued under the leadership of Judas and, after him, two of his brothers. Independence was not achieved until 142 B.C. The Hasmonean period, as it is called, lasted from 163 to 134 B.C.[3] and was the last period of Jewish political independence until the establishment of the State of Israel in A.D. 1948. At its greatest extent, in the time of Alexander Jannaeus (103–76 B.C.), the kingdom included all of Palestine north of Beersheba—except the district round Ascalon and the coastal area north of Mount Carmel—and also a very large part of western Transjordan north of the River Zered (Wadi al-Hasa). It was not, however, a truly happy period because it was marred by both internal and external strife.

Internally the opposition developed because the Hasmonean rulers took for themselves the offices of both king and high priest and were accused by the Pharisees, sincerely anxious to remain faithful to true Judaism, of being arrogant and licentious. Nor were the Pharisees the only people to be offended and rebellion broke out against Alexander Jannaeus, which he suppressed with the utmost cruelty though it took him six years to do so. After his death there developed a bitter struggle for power in the Hasmonean family. The external struggle was with the growing power of the Nabateans, with their capital at Petra.

In 63 B.C. the Romans intervened directly in Palestinian affairs when Pompey captured Jerusalem and, to the horror of the Jews, strode into

---

2. An excellent brief introduction to this period is D. S. Russell, *Between the Testaments* (Philadelphia: Fortress Press, 1960).

3. The five Hasmonean rulers were in fact members of the Maccabean family but the title "Maccabeus" ("hammer") is normally reserved for Judas and his two brothers.

the Temple and even into the Holy of Holies. For the next seven hundred years Palestine was part of the Roman Empire. At first they dominated the country through local rulers, of whom the most famous is Herod the Great (37–4 B.C.). A brilliant but ruthless ruler, he is celebrated certainly for his rebuilding of the Jerusalem Temple on a grandiose scale but he was no less ready to build pagan sanctuaries, such as the Temple of Jupiter at Samaria which he renamed Sebaste, and so prove his loyalty to Rome. Severe rioting followed his death and was suppressed with great brutality by his son Archelaus, whose rule was so intolerable that the Romans banished him and for the next sixty years governed Judea directly through a Roman procurator.[4]

HELLENISTIC PALESTINE

During all this turbulent period the traditional life of the village farmers and shepherds, as well as that of the nomadic or seminomadic Bedouin, continued unchanged from the days of the monarchy and indeed persisted until the early years of our own century. But the increasing domination of the whole Levant by Hellenistic culture brought about striking changes in the general appearance of the country. The small towns of the past, with narrow streets and houses huddled closely together within the protection of high walls, gave place to much larger, carefully planned cities, with long colonnaded streets, theaters, public baths, and Greek-style temples. The incorporation of Palestine and Syria into a huge imperial system required better communications by both land and sea, although the building of sturdy highways of stone with regular milestones did not come about until the Roman period. The Mediterranean port cities grew in size and new ports such as Caesarea, built by Herod the Great, came into existence because of the necessity of frequent communication with Greece and Rome. This communication was, however, suspended during the winter months, because of the danger of destructive storms, one of which is vividly described in Acts 27.[5]

---

4. The one exception was from A.D. 41 to 44 when Herod's grandson, Herod Agrippa I, was King of Judea. This is the Herod mentioned in Acts 12:1, 20–23.

5. The fast mentioned in verse 9 is Yom Kippur (the Day of Atonement), which falls in either late September or early October.

NEW TESTAMENT PALESTINE

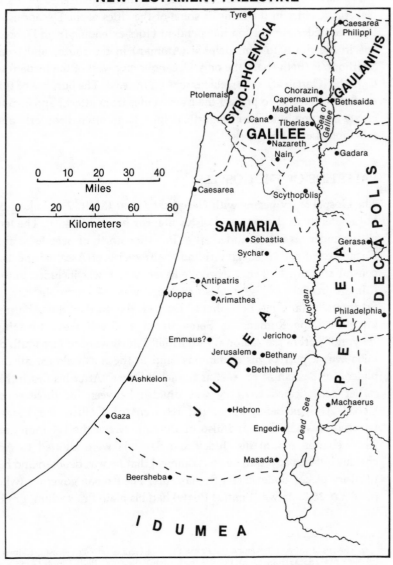

We have vivid evidence still today of the magnificence of these Hellenistic cities in the ruins of some of the cities of the Decapolis, a loose confederation of ten independent cities extending from Damascus in the north to Philadelphia (Amman) in the south, and from Scythopolis (Beth-shan, the only Decapolis city west of the Jordan) to Canatha (Qanawat) in the Jebel Druze on the east. The purpose of this confederation was to protect the trade routes from attack, and also to create a strong block of Hellenistic culture in an often disorderly and rebellious Levantine world.[6]

PALESTINE OF THE GOSPELS

The Gospel story begins with Herod the Great (Matt. 2:1; Luke 1:5) but evidently at the very end of his life, for he died in 4 B.C. The territory under his rule included all of Palestine north of Beersheba and Gaza, except for an enclave round the free city of Ascalon and the coastal area north of the Crocodile River, which was included in the Roman province of Syria. Also excluded was the Decapolis city of Scythopolis (ancient Beth-shan). East of the Jordan the Abarim, known to the Romans as Perea (from a Greek word meaning "beyond"), from the Arnon (Wadi Mojjib) northward to just south of Pella was a part of his dominions, and in the north almost all the plateau of Bashan as far east as the Jebel Druze. After his death this rather complicated territory was divided between his three sons, Herod Antipas being appointed tetrarch[7] of Galilee and Perea, tetrarch of all Bashan and also of Iturea between the Lebanon and Anti-Lebanon mountains. Judea and Samaria were allotted to Archelaus but he proved to be so tyrannical that he was deposed and his territory placed under direct Roman rule. The Roman governor (who from A.D. 26 to 36 was Pontius Pilate) had his main Praetorium, or of-

---

6. The finest ruins still existing today are those of Gerasa (modern Jerash), followed by those of Gadara (Umm Qeis), Pella in the Jordan Valley, and Philadelphia (Amman), the southernmost of the Decapolis cities.

7. A tetrarch in the Roman system was the ruler over a smaller area than that of a king, and with somewhat more restricted authority. The title seems, however, to have been somewhat fluid and sometimes a tetrarch was spoken of as king, perhaps out of flattery.

ficial residence, at the port city of Caesarea but a secondary one in Jerusalem. This was the political situation in the time of Jesus' ministry.[8]

The Gospels mention surprisingly few places in their account of Jesus' life and ministry and some of these cannot be identified with certainty. Except for Jerusalem none of them was a major city. Bethlehem, his birthplace, and Nazareth, his home, were little more than villages, and so were Cana in Galilee (John 2:1; 5:46), Nain, where he raised the widow's son (Luke 7:11), and Bethany and Bethphage close to Jerusalem (Matt. 21:17; 26:6; Mark 11:1-12; 14:3; Luke 19:29; 24:50; John 11:1, 18; 12:1). Capernaum on the northwest shore of the Lake of Galilee and the main center of Jesus' ministry, Chorazin overlooking the lake from the basalt plateau to the north, and Bethsaida were all important enough to be called towns. Unfortunately, we are still in the dark about the exact site of Bethsaida, although three of Jesus' disciples are said to have come from there (Andrew, Peter, and Philip; John 1:44; 12:21) and we are told that much of Jesus' work was done in Bethsaida and Chorazin (Matt. 11:20-24; Luke 10:13-15). There was certainly a town (later dignified as a city) called Bethsaida-Julias east of the the lake and therefore in Gentile territory, but we do not know exactly where it was. Moreover, Bethsaida is said by John to have been in Galilee.[9] Some scholars have argued for two Bethsaidas, one east and one west of the lake, which is certainly possible but not altogether probable. Others suggest that "in Galilee" in John refers to the region immediately surrounding the lake, another distinct possibility, but no less lacking in proof.

It is admittedly disappointing to have so little certainty about the actual places in which Jesus taught and did his mighty works, but the writers of the Gospels did not necessarily ask the kind of questions

---

8. See Luke 3:1 for the political distribution, and Matt. 27:27; Mark 15;16; John 18:28, 33; 19:9; Acts 23:35 for the Praetorium, sometimes translated "judgment hall." The identification of the "pavement," or courtyard of the Praetorium, in John 19:13 with the impressive Roman pavement below the Convent of the Sisters of Zion north of the Temple Area must now, alas, be rejected, since this pavement is now known to belong to a later period.

9. See John 1:44; 12:21. Bethsaida-Julias is usually identified with et-Tell, 2 miles (3 km) north of the lake and close to the River Jordan, but as yet we have no proof.

that we would like to have answered. For them the question was never "Where exactly did this happen?" but "In what territory did this take place, and what significance does this territory have?" They undoubtedly knew the Scriptures, i.e., the Old Testament, and saw the whole life of Jesus as the fulfillment of those Scriptures. Jerusalem was for them the Holy City, and the Temple its sacred center. If they speak of things happening in the "wilderness," they have in mind the story of the Exodus. They were well aware that for all orthodox Jews the Samaritans signified the "quislings," who were held to have betrayed true Judaism and deserted the faith. There was even a great temple of Jupiter in the city of Sebaste, once called Samaria. East of the Jordan was for them barbarian and pagan country even though in fact it did have Jewish inhabitants, although probably not a great number of them. When, therefore, a multitude are fed in the wilderness east of the Jordan (Matt. 15:32–39; Mark 8:1–10; John 6:1–14), it is the despised Gentiles who are understood to have shared the Exodus experience, and therefore to be now no longer regarded as barbarians but as fit to be fellow citizens of the Kingdom. It was certainly inevitable, men and women being what they are, that quite early in Christian history the faithful should want to go in pilgrimage to places associated with Jesus in the days of his ministry but the Gospel writers wrote with another aim in mind. Their purpose was to proclaim that there was now a new Creation, open to all and sundry—pagans and Samaritans no less than the Jewish people themselves.

SUGGESTIONS
FOR FURTHER
READING

N.B. All the books listed here are valuable but unfortunately not all are still in print. However, they should be available in any good library.

Aharoni, Yohanan. *The Land of the Bible: A Historical Geography.* Translated and edited by A. F. Rainey. Philadelphia: Westminster Press, 1979.

Aharoni, Yohanan, and Michael Avi-Yonah. *The Macmillan Bible Atlas.* New York: Macmillan Co., 1977.

Baly, Denis. *The Geography of the Bible.* New York: Harper & Row, 1974.

Baly, Denis, and A. D. Tushingham. *Atlas of the Biblical World.* New York: World Publishing Company, 1971.

Cleave, Richard. *The Historical Map Manual: Historical Geography of Bible Lands.* Edited by J. Monson et al. Grand Rapids: Zondervan, 1980.

May, Herbert G. *Oxford Bible Atlas.* Revised for the third edition by John Day. New York: Oxford University Press, 1984.

Orni, Efraim, and Elisha Ofrat. *Geography of Israel.* Fourth Revised Edition. Jerusalem: Israel Universities Press, 1980.

Van der Woude, A. S., general editor. *The World of the Bible.* Translated by Sierd Woudstra. Grand Rapids: Wm. B. Eerdmans, 1986.

The *Oxford Bible Atlas* is probably the easiest for the ordinary reader to use since it is clear, well researched, and covers the entire Middle East. Also strongly recommended are the large *Atlas of Israel* and the *Atlas of Jordan*, of which so far only the first volume has appeared, on Climate and Agroclimatology.

SUBJECT INDEX

SUBJECT INDEX

SUBJECT INDEX

Parthians, 11
Passover, 30
Patriarchs, 51, 52
Paul, Saint, 47
Pella, 72
Penuel, 61
Perea, 72
Persia, 68n
Persian Empire, 68
Persian Gulf, 7
Petra, 16, 65, 67, 69
Pharisees, 69
Philadelphia, 72
Phoenicia, 16
Pomegranate, 32
Pompey, 11, 69
Pontic Mountains, 7
Pontius Pilate, 72
Praetorium, 73 n.8
Pride of Jordan, 55
Ptolemais, 45, 50
Ptolemies, 11, 68
Punon, 56, 65
Pyrenees, 7

Qanawat, 72
Qasr al-ʿAbd, 62
Qattara, 55
Qilt, Wadi, 52
Qumran, 55

Rabbah of the Am-
    monites (see Rabboth
    Ammon)
Rabboth Ammon (see
    also Amman), 7, 61,
    63, 66
Rain, 14, 16, 20, 21,
    22–25, 31, 45, 55, 61,
    66
Rameses III, 48
Rams, 59
Ras an-Naqb, 66
Red Sea, 11, 12, 15, 56
Refugees, 34
Reuben, 62
Richard I of England, 49
Rift Valley, Central (see
    also Jordan-Arabah
    Rift Valley) 14, 15, 18,
    22, 30
Rift Valleys, 12
Roads, 17
Roebuck, 35
Rome, Romans, 67, 69,
    72
Rosh ha-ʿAyin, 47
Rosh ha-Shanah, 25

Sahara Desert, 7

Salekah, 61
Salkhad, 61
Samaria, Samaritans, 34,
    51, 70, 72, 74
Samson, 49
Sandstone, 66
Sassanids, 11
Scythopolis, 72
Sea Peoples, 48
Sebaste, 70, 74
Sebkha, 56
Seleucids, 11, 68
Senonian chalk, 17, 49,
    50
Sepphoris, 50
Shaghur fault, 49
Sharon, Plain of, 15
Shechem, 50
Sheep, 14, 27, 32–33, 34,
    50, 51, 53
Shephelah, 49
Shepherd, 28–29, 30, 70
Sidon, 12, 14
Sihon, 62
Sinai, 9
Sirocco, 26
Snow, 20, 22, 23, 24, 61,
    65, 66
Sodom, 56
Solomon, King (see also
    King Solomon's
    mines), 32, 35, 56
Sorek, 49
Southland, 15
Spring (season), 21,
    25–26
Spring (water), 66–67
Storms, 20, 23, 64, 70
Succoth, 25
Syria, 11, 12, 72
Syro-Phoenician Realm,
    14

Tafileh, 65
Taurus Mountains, 7
Tell ʿAshtarah, 61
Tell el-Fukhkhar, 45
Temple, general, 70
Temple, Jerusalem, 34,
    69, 70, 74
Theaters, 70
Thunder, 23
Tiberias, 24, 50, 54, 55
Tien Shan, 7
Tobiah the Servant, 62
Tophel, 65
Trade route, 47, 51,
    66–67
Traders, 16, 59, 64–65

Transitional seasons,
    25–26
Transjordan, 15, 17, 21,
    24, 69, 74
Tsinling Shan, 7
Tulūl adh-Dhahab, 59
    n.1, 61
Turkey, 7, 9, 28, 29
Tyre, 14, 16, 26

Ugarit, 14
Umm Qeis, 72 n.6
Uzziah, King, 17, 56

Vegetables, 61
Vine, vineyards (see also
    Grapes), 25, 30–31, 52,
    61

Wadi Ram, 66
Wadi Ytem, 66
Wala, river, 59
Warrior, 59
Wells, 66–67
Western Highlands, 15
Wheat, 14, 48, 59, 61,
    62, 63
Wilderness, 33–35, 50
Wilderness, The (see
    also Jeshimon), 52–53,
    74
Wind, 56
Winter (wet season), 21,
    22–24
Wolf, 35, 64
Woods (see also Forest;
    Yaʿar), 33–35, 50,
    64

Yaʿar (see also Forest;
    Woods), 34–35
Yarmuq, battle of, 11
Yarmuq, River, 11, 12,
    57
Yom Kippur, 25, 70 n.5

Zagros Mountains, 7, 11
Zered, River, 12, 59, 63,
    69
Zerqa, River, 59, 61
Zerqa (town), 61
Zerqa Maʿin 56

78

SCRIPTURE INDEX

SCRIPTURE INDEX